The Betrayal of Dr. Babasaheb Ambedkar

The Betrayal of Dr. Babasaheb Ambedkar

Sheshrao Chavan

AUTHORSPRESS
Publishers of Scholarly Books

Worldwide Circulation through Authorspress Global Network

First Published 2011
by
Authorspress

Editorial
Q-2A Hauz Khas Enclave,
New Delhi-110 016
e-mail: authorspress@yahoo.com

Marketing
E-35/103, Jawahar Park
Laxmi Nagar, Delhi-110 092
e-mail: authorspress@yahoo.com

The Betrayal of Dr. Babasaheb Ambedkar
ISBN 978-81-7273-609-5

Printed in India at Tarun Offset, Delhi.

I do not pray for my soul. I am a Buddhist.

Nobody needs trouble of praying for my soul.

I do not believe in God. I have no soul.

I have spared you that trouble.

Dr. B.R.Ambedkar

Foreword

It gives me great pleasure in writing a Foreword to this informative book written by Shri Sheshrao Chavan. The title of this book, *Betrayal of Dr. Babasaheb Ambedkar* is an quite eloquent and speaking one. It speaks volumes.

I had the privilege of meeting Dr. Babasaheb Ambedkar, when my father was a Member of the Constituent Assembly. I had also the privilege of witnessing Dhamma Chakra Pravartan Ceremony when Dr. Babasaheb Ambedkar embraced Buddhism, with thousands of his followers at Nagpur. I was then a practising lawyer at Nagpur and many of his followers were my personal friends. In my opinion Dhamma Chakra Pravartan Ceremony, which was a mass conversion, was a historic one, in several senses.

There is a sentence from the life of Jesus Christ, which says: "Not knowing how to punish great men for their greatness fate punishes them by giving them disciples. Disciples are not successors. The successors have proud privilege to take one step forward, and followers have neither courage nor capacity to do so. A successor is also a path finder, as they start from where Guru had to stop."

The conversion in the life of Dr. Babasaheb Ambedkar was not an accident, but he was rather forced by the circumstances to get himself converted into Buddhism. In Hindu religion, caste is a reality and religion is a fiction, or we may call it, it is the total of caste and sub-castes. A person cannot be a Hindu, unless he belongs to a particular caste. You cannot deny your caste because it is based on birth and you cannot change your birth or parents. Caste is exclusive. The characteristic of a caste is that it has only one door, i.e., the door for exit. It has no door for entrance, except by birth. The second characteristic of the caste is that it shuns human contacts, so the caste system is anti-social. A person who is in a disadvantageous position in the caste system, he has no other alternative except to change his religion.

Dr. Babasaheb Ambedkar was born as an untouchable. Untouchables had no respect, dignity or status in Hindu society. Therefore, the only alternative before him was to get converted to some other religion. In his religious conversion, there is also patriotic feeling, as well as the feeling of national integration. There are several religions in India—Christian, Muslim, Sikh, Buddhism and others, but from all these religions, Dr. Babasaheb Ambedkar chose to get converted to Buddhism, because that was the most suited to the Indian culture, and was in harmony with the Indian mind.

What is culture? Culture is an art of living with others and this relationship is the essence of cultural attitude. The relationship precludes alienation of all kinds. So a person like Dr. Babasaheb Ambedkar blazed the trend by accepting Buddhism, which, according to me, is an act of patriotism and national integration.

There is a saying that, "To be a Great is to be misunderstood." This is practically true about every great man and particularly about Mahatma Gandhi and Dr. Babasaheb Ambedkar. If he (Dr. Ambedkar) would have lived for a few more years, I am sure, it would have made a great difference. He himself had said that, if he had some more years to go, he would fulfil the task he had undertaken to a great extent, but alas, that was not to happen.

There is lot of misunderstanding about this mass conversion, which is known as Dhamma Chakra Pravartan. This misunderstanding is the result of ignorance. In my opinion, it was a concrete step taken by Dr. Babasaheb Ambedkar towards nationalism and national integration. This is required to be understood by everybody in its proper perspective. In India, a person acquires his caste in the womb of his or her mother, it cannot be renounced, nor does it end with death. A person takes birth with the particular caste label and dies with the same label. That is why even after death, we do not allow persons belonging to other castes to touch the dead body. Another feature of the caste is alienation. Purity of a person depends upon this alienation. As if this is not enough, there is a ruling race in this caste system. Dr. Babasaheb Ambedkar had said, "Hindu religion is a four-storeyed building; a person who is born on a particular floor, is forced to live on that floor and also forced to die there, since there is no ladder or staircase to go from one floor to another. "Therefore, a person who has no honourable place in Hindu society, who receives no dignified treatment, from other castes, has no other alternative but to get converted into other religion. Though Dr. Babasaheb Ambedkar was a highly educated person and had travelled worldwide, because of the caste system, he had no dignified place in Hindu society.

Unfortunately, there are people in India who still want to defend the caste system in one name or another. Today the electoral merit of a candidate depends upon his caste. In the Indian Constitution, it is solemnly declared that, "Untouchability" is abolished and its practice in any form is forbidden. The enforcement of any disability arising out of "Untouchability" "shall be an offence punishable in accordance with law." A particular name of the caste of an untouchable is also abolished, and now they are known as Scheduled Castes. But untouchability still prevails in Hindu mind and it is practised indirectly. Several villages in the country are still divided on the caste basis. Even after several years of independence, we have not been able to change the social map of the villages or towns. There is also confusion and misunderstanding about the expressions of caste and class.

The following observations made by Shri P.B. Gajendragadkar, former Chief Justice of India, in this context, are very significant:

"The groups of citizens to whom Article 15 (4) applies, are described as classes of citizens and not as castes of citizens. A class, according to the dictionary meaning, shows division of society according to the status, rank or caste. In the Hindu social structure, caste unfortunately plays an important part in determining the status of citizens. Though according to sociologists and Vedic scholars, the caste system may have originally begun as an occupational or functional basis, in course of time it became rigid and inflexible. The history of the growth of the caste system shows that its original functional and occupational basis was later overburdened with considerations of purity based on ritual concepts, and that led to its ramifications which introduced inflexibility and rigidity. The artificial growth inevitably tended to create a feeling of superiority and inferiority and to foster narrow caste loyalties. Therefore, in dealing with this question as to whether a class of citizens is socially backward or not, it may not be irrelevant to consider the caste of the said group of citizens. Social backwardness is the ultimate analysis of the result of poverty to a very large extent. The classes of citizens who are deplorably poor, automatically become socially backward. They do not enjoy a status in society and have, therefore, to be content to take a backward seat. It is true that social backwardness which results from poverty is likely to be aggravated by considerations of caste to which poor citizens may belong, but that only shows the relevance of both caste and poverty in determining the backwardness of citizens.

"The occupations of citizens may also contribute to make classes of citizens socially backward. There are some occupations which are treated as inferior according to conventional beliefs and classes of citizens who follow these occupations are apt to become socially backward. The place of habitation also plays not a minor part in determining the backwardness of a community of persons. In a sense, the problem of social backwardness is the problem of rural India and in that behalf, classes of citizens occupying a socially backward position in rural areas fall within the purview of Article 15 (4)." (M. R. Balaji vs. The State of Mysore, AIR 1963 Supreme Court 649).

In order to enable these backward classes to achieve rapid material progress, various state governments have been giving them different kinds of special concessions. These concessions are meant for equalization of the starting point. An unfortunate development is the desperate tendency of practically every caste to get itself included in the list of backward castes. This is an indication of the obvious fact that the entire country is backward. But this tendency is not as harmless as it seems on the surface. When one sees the keen competition amongst various castes to establish their backwardness in the eye of the law, one naturally gets suspicious about their bona fides. We had to make special provisions in the Constitution for the backward tribes and castes because the rest of the community does not feel that it is duty-bound to help these backward sections of our society.

Dr. Babasaheb Ambedkar tried his level best for the upliftment of the untouchables, but his efforts proved to be an exercise in futility. Therefore, he had no other alternative left but to renounce Hinduism and embrace Buddhism. In his address, at the time of Dhamma Chakra Pravartan, he said: "Unfortunately, Hinduism, which is based on ideologies of inequality and injustice, leaves no room for development of the untouchables; they continue to be slaves and cannot hope for better life of status and dignity." According to him Buddha Religion was based on equality. It was based on ethical principles. Buddha was not a God in himself, but acted as Guide. Buddhism is not idol worshiper, as is the case with other religions. Though Buddha and his religion do not believe in idolism, today maximum idols are of Buddha in the world. But the tragedy is that after conversion, a new sect and name came into existence, known as Neo-Buddhists.

There are some people who say Ambedkar was not patriotic. They do not seem to have understood him. Ambedkar was every inch a patriot and a nationalist, which is evident from what he said in 1938 on the Bill for the creation of a separate Karnataka province. "I want all people to be Indians first, Indians last and nothing else but Indians." The Constitution of India is an outcome of this patriotism. In his last speech this is what he observed:

"We must make our political democracy a social democracy as well. Political democracy cannot last unless there lies at the base of it social democracy. What does social democracy mean? It means a way of life which recognizes liberty, equality and fraternity as the principles of life. These principles of liberty, equality fraternity are not to be treated as separate items in a trinity. They form a union of trinity in the sense that to divorce one from the other is to defeat the very purpose of democracy. Liberty cannot be divorced from equality. Equality cannot be divorced from liberty. Nor can liberty and equality be divorced from fraternity. Without equality, liberty would produce the supremacy of the few over the many. Equality without liberty would kill individual initiative. Without fraternity, liberty and equality cannot become a natural course of things. It would require a constable to enforce them. We must begin by acknowledging the fact that there is complete absence of two things in Indian society. One of these is equality. On the social plane, we have in India a society based on the principle of graded inequality which means elevation for some and degradation for others. On the economic plane, we have a society in which there are some who have immense wealth as against many who live in abject poverty. On the 26th of January, 1950, we are going to enter into a life of contradictions. In politics we will have equality, and in social and economic life we will have inequality. In politics we will be recognizing the principle of one man one-vote and one-vote, one value. In our social and economic life, we shall, by reason of our social and economic structure, continue to deny the principle of one man-one value. How long shall we continue to live this life of contradictions? How long shall we continue to deny equality in our social and economic life? If we continue to deny it for long, we will do so only by putting our political democracy in peril. We must remove this contradiction at the earliest possible moment or else those who suffer from inequality will blow up the structure of political democracy which this Assembly has so laboriously built up".

In my opinion, unfortunately, because of his early death, he could not implement his thoughts and values in the Indian society. Our society is full of inconsistencies and contradictions. He had no successor, but only followers or disciples who were not able to go ahead or improve upon his thinking. That is why Shri Sheshrao Chavan had to call it a "Betrayal" for which all other caste people are also responsible.

We could not understand the very concept of Brotherhood and Equality and the fact that every Fundamental Right carries with it the corresponding Duty, rather, Right cannot exist without corresponding Duty, rather rights are conferred for the fulfilment of the Duties. Therefore, by amending the Constitution, the chapter relating to Fundamental Duties and, particularly Article 51A, was inserted in the Constitution. Some of the clauses of this Article are very important and speaking, such as Clause (c), Clause (e), Clause (f), and Clause (h), which are reproduced below:

> It shall be the duty of every citizen of India:
>
> c) to uphold and protect the sovereignty, unity and integrity of India;
>
> e) to promote harmony and the spirit of common brotherhood amongst all the people of India transcending religious, linguistic and regional or sectional diversities, to renounce practices derogatory to the dignity of women;
>
> f) to value and preserve the rich heritage of our composite culture;
>
> h) to develop the scientific temper, humanism and the spirit of inquiry and reform...

The original Constitution was required to be amended to make explicit, which was implicit, in Preamble and various other chapters of the Constitution. This clearly indicates our failure and betrayal towards the thoughts and values, as propagated by Dr. Ambedkar. As well said by the famous philosopher Khalil Gibran: "As a single leaf turn not yellow but with the silent knowledge of the whole tree, so the wrong-doer cannot do wrong without the hidden will of you all." Thus all of us are responsible for the betrayal of Dr. Ambedkar, as well as his rise and fall.

One may agree or may have a different opinion about the views expressed by the author, but it is clear that these views require serious consideration and cannot be brushed aside easily. It is well said: "That understanding the Problems is the beginning of its Solution." And there are no ready-made answers or solutions for it. The least I expect from the readers is to consider and appreciate the views expressed in this book in a fair and judicious manner. To say the least, I have great admiration and appreciation for this book. In my opinion, Shri Sheshrao Chavan has done a yeoman service by writing this book, which will help to remove several misunderstandings about Dr. Babasaheb Ambedkar. I wish the book every success.

Padmabhushan Justice Chandrashekhar Dharmadhikari

Former Judge, Bombay High Court

Preface

When Kaka, as we affectionately call Shesharaoji Chavan, talked to me in his study about the subject matter of the book for the first time a cord of concord was struck in my heart. I was looking forward for the book to be ready, as I then felt that it was inordinately overdue. Finally I got it in my hand in August 2010 and I went through it quickly. I was amazed to see the depth of understanding of the author and his ability to lay bare the facts concerning the betrayal of Dr. Ambedkar which none, according to my knowledge, among staunch Buddhists or Ambedkarites, ever dared to touch. Not only that that but also none even dreamt of the gravity of the post-Ambedkar situation of his movement and tried to know how Dr. Ambedkar's ideal has been distorted and made mockery of by his followers. I congratulate the author for producing in all sincerity a bold and useful book. In his efforts in diagnosing the ailing Dhamma-kranti, i.e., Revolution by way of the Dhamma, of Dr. Ambedkar what a hard labour, both physical and intellectual, is put into the task by the author! If there is no diagnosis of the malady, the remedy is not possible. Similarly, if there is no understanding of the present state of Ambedkarite movement, no measures can be taken to help it. As this study is done by a non-Buddhist author whose approach is dispassionate and impartial, that makes this work really worthwhile. This book should be an eye-opener not only to the Ambedkarites but also to all intellectuals in India who bother to see the nation rise to its lost ancient glory once again.

Dr. Ambedkar had said, 'I will make the whole of India Buddhist." As a matter of fact, no doubt, it sounded to be an impossible task. It was easy for many to draw a hasty conclusion labeling it as a boastful utterance or wishful thinking on the part of Dr. Ambedkar. But if we look closely enough at Dr. Ambedkar's life which was full of abuses, insults, and injustice they were sufficient to turn any person bitter and revengeful. But he refrained from ill-will and hatred toward the perpetrators, and instead cultivated profound love and compassion for welfare and happiness of all people in India which is nothing less than sainthood. That is why he is called a Bodhisattva, which means one who is firmly established on the path of enlightenment. He was convinced that the teachings of the Buddha were alone capable of saving one and all in India. So instead of helping his own community or only the backward communities with Dhamma, he wished all Indians to be Buddhist. Therefore, I think, instead of considering his slogan of making India Buddhist a boastful or wishful thinking, it could be viewed as his gesture of compassionate intention without any trace of malice towards anyone, whether he himself could have accomplished it or not, but from his point of view that was surely the only way that he was keen on to point out.

The revival of Buddhism in India by Dr. Ambedkar was an epoch-making event in modern Indian history, the parallel of which can only be found in Emperor Ashoka's quest for

Dhamma-vijaya in ancient India. However, considering the multiplicity of sects and diversity in forms of Buddhism that were prevalent at the time, Dr. Ambedkar wanted to go back to the original teachings of the Buddha, which could be traced in all sects, and thus he advocated non-sectarian approach to Buddhism.

At the same time the absorption of the Buddha and some of his best teaching by Hinduism had created a lot of confusion in understanding the Buddha and his Dhamma which called for immediate clearance. The present writer has quoted extensively from repudiate scholars, both Eastern and Western, in support of the universal appreciation of the Buddha and His Dhamma. Yet a majority of Indian people are apathetic to Buddhism for reasons of unclear distinction of Buddhism from Hinduism. To deal with this problem Dr. Ambedkar wrote his famous magnum opum *The Buddha and His Dhamma.* He also administrated 22 Vows to the newly converted Buddhists. so as to protect them from being confused. He made clear the difference between Religion (or Dharma) and the Dhamma using the original term in Pali language and also explained the true import of the Buddha's teaching in terms of Saddhamma. In the words of Bhikkhu Narada: "The original term for Buddhism is Dhamma, which, literally means that which upholds or sustains (him who acts in conformity with its principles and thus prevents him from falling into woeful states). There is no proper English equivalent that exactly conveys the meaning of the Pali term. Similarly, the term 'Dharma' in Sanskrit is also inappropriate.

"The Dhamma is that which really is. It is the Doctrine of Reality. It is a Means of Deliverance from suffering and

Deliverance itself. Whether the Buddhas arise or not the Dhamma exists from all eternity. It is a Buddha that realizes this Dhamma, which ever lies hidden from the ignorant eyes of men, till He, an enlightened One, comes and compassionately reveals it to the world." (Narada, *The Buddha and His Teachings*, Malaysia, 4th Ed. 1988, pp-295-6)

But the confusion created, upheld and ceaselessly propagated by subordination of Buddhism to Hinduism by the Hindu scholarship which is deep rooted in Hindu psyche is yet another headache today. Dr. Ambedkar did not find time to deal with this nuisance. The Brahmin scholars such as Swami Vivekananda, Dr. Radhakishnan and Dr. P.V. Kane, Jawaharlal Nehru and others, and for that matter even the Western scholars like Mrs. Rhys David and others being only rationalists and not practical Buddhists, consistently held that the Buddha was Hindu and stated that he was 'a rebel child of Hinduism' or 'reformer of Hinduism', and what's more, have thought of Buddhism as ever existing Hinduism, the teachings of which have been drawn from the *Vedas* and *Upanishads* etc. Some light needs to be shed on this for better understanding of the present book.

As regards Nehru's knowledge of Buddhism, it was derived from second-hand modern books by Indian writers of the Brahmanical school and European writers of Older Anglo-German School. Much of what he says, however, is in conformity with the views of Swami Vivekananda (Joshi, p.72). In so far as his view about the antiquity of Vedic age is concerned one must note that the Jains and Buddhists both cherish the legends of twenty-three past Jinas before Mahavir and twenty-four (or eight?) Buddhas before the Sakyamuni Buddha. It is impossible to establish their historical existence, but their names exist. And also an inscription of third century B.C. celebrates a stupa of Kanakamuni Buddha. The historical Sakyamuni Buddha continued the ancient religious tradition of non-Aryan and non-Vedic *munis* and *sramanas (pubbakehei sammasambuddhehi)* as told by the Buddha himself in *Nagarasutta* (S.N..II. pp-90-91) Therefore, Vedic antiquity is not applicable to Buddhism and hence, not acceptable.

In this respect Lal Mani Joshi (pp.37-8) has rightly observed, "The use of the word 'Hindu' in the study of ancient Indian History and culture is wrong. This word means simply an Indian; anyone who is born and lives in Hind or Hindustan or India is a Hindu. The use of this geographical term for a religious affiliation is rooted in confusion. Those who are now called Hindus follow the Vedic-Brahmanic traditions; they are the followers either of Vaishnavism of Shaivism or Shaktism or a mixed religion, a mélange of several diverse elements of Vedic and Puranic origin. A substantial portion of what is now known as Hinduism is the contribution of Buddhism and Jainism, Yoga and Samkhya, and of many other thought-currents of non-Vedic and non-Aryan origins. The worship of Shiva, Shakti, Ganesha, Hauman, serpent (*naga*), trees (i.e. *pipala*) and the several aspects of the theology of Vishnu are of non-Aryan and non-Vedic origin.

"However, the use of the word 'Hinduism' for the composite religious mélange, which is now only nominally related to Vedic tradition, has become widespread. What is important to remember is that the modern Hindu like this name, although in the entire mass of ancient literature belonging to the Vedic-Brahmanic sects, such as the Vaidika, Vedantika, Aupanishadika, Mimansaka, Shaiva, Bhagavata, Vaishnava, Shakta, Ganapatya, Saura, Shrauta, Smarta, Pauranika, Tantrika etc. nowhere do we come across the word 'Hindu' in a religious or a sectarian sense before the coming of the Muslims. In our opinion the use of the word Hinduism for any sect or group of sects of ancient India is anachronistic and unscientific." Thus, it shows not only a blatant hollowness of the Hindu scholars but also their undue haughtiness toward the Buddha and his Dhamma. This being the fact, one wonders why the best brains of so-called Hinduism sing the same song. It may be out of love for their own creed or failure in understanding the Buddha and his Dhamma.

The subject matter of the so-called Hinduism or Vaidikism or all other religions or sects is completely different and far removed from that of Buddhism. Moreover, in order to understand Buddhism, one must see Buddhism as a Buddhist sees it. The Hindu scholarship failed to do so. So whatever they have to say in respect of Buddhism is one-sided view in frantic efforts of proving the Vedic origin of Buddhism and superiority of its present form of Hinduism rather than an honest understanding and appreciation of Buddhism.

Explaining the heart of Buddhism, in their book *What is Reality?* (*Sri Lanka 2010,* pp.245, 248-250) Dhammadassi Bhikkhu and Kenneth B.Gunatunge, have to say his: "Young Siddhartha set forth alone over 2500 years ago in the search of deathlessness, nothing less, a thing hitherto unknown, unheard of and never unmasked; and what's more, never even thought of as ever existing. Siddhartha wanted to find this deathlessness in its totality, and nothing else mattered to him even going to heavenly realms and having a blissful life there!

"In the process of attaining a super concentrated mind, Prince Siddhartha had to stop all inputs from, i.e., six senses, namely, eye, ear, nose, tongue, the physical body and the mind itself. Hence, all perceptions flowing in through the six senses were stopped. He came to a stage where, although no perceptions were coming through the six senses, yet, there was perception in him. So, Prince Siddhartha as a lonely explorer used his super-concentrated mind to produce thought waves of laser gun calibre to look inwards into his own mind/body mechanism,

"He explored, investigated, studied and analyzed in microscopic details the characteristics, functions, operation procedures and indeed every aspect of his mind/body mechanism. For example, let us take the case of seeing through the eye. He found that when an external object comes into the vicinity of the eye, consciousness arises. And through the contact of these three (the external object, eye and the eye consciousness) perception occurs followed by feelings, thinking, etc., through to the stages of cognizance and the final formation of concepts. He found how the concepts that formed were totally dependent on our memory-bank of knowledge, experience, biases, and earlier judgements etc. which were in turn based on purely the information gained from the world outside, through the six senses. He applied the same process for all other senses, the ear, nose, tongue etc. and analyzed them in microscopic details.

"In this process of microscopic examination and analysis, Prince Siddhartha had to penetrate many barriers of biases, prejudices, opinions and views, etc., that were tightly held by his own mind to unmask the reality of this natural phenomenon of mind/body activity. In this process of microscopic examination and analysis, Prince Siddhartha used his new-found tool, the super-concentration of mind to uproot one by one his worldly knowledge, experiences, biases, prejudices, judgements and attachments of al kinds, totally out of his mind. His mind became pure with a purity of a quality unknown before. Surrounding this purity was wisdom; a new kind of wisdom that could penetrate through the veil of our worldly know-how, beliefs, views and habits and see the true nature of all phenomena. This is called the 'penetrative wisdom', the only wisdom that can help one to realize the true nature of reality through experiential understanding.

"Thus he became the knower of what reality really is. Light arose in him, darkness was expelled, and the experiential knowledge of true reality marked the end of his worldly journey with no turning back to the old fold and thus he was carried to a supreme state of deathlessness never known before. Thus, Prince Siddhartha became the Buddha, the discoverer of the true nature of all phenomena and the conqueror of deathlessness. And he transcended the world, the world and its concomitants that we are so familiar with throughout our lives. He became a man 'of the world' but 'not in the world'. This last sentence has a far deeper meaning attached to it then meets the eye."

This deathlessness is celled "Nibbana". The Buddha discovered without any trace of doubt that it is the weaving of the worldly life and its continuum based on desire, lust, greed, hate and delusion. This last line of explanation has great significance in the entire doctrine of the Buddha."

Bhikkhu Narada has observed: "A purely intellectual comprehension of Nibbana is impossible because it is not a matter to be arrived at by logical reasoning (*atakkavacara*). The words of the Buddha are perfectly logical, but *Nibbana*, the ultimate goal of Buddhism, is beyond the scope of logic. Nevertheless, by reflecting on the positive and negative aspects of life, the logical conclusion emerges that in contradistinction to a conditioned phenomenal existence, there must exist a sorrow less, deathless, non-conditioned State."

All this is beyond the gambit of Vedic and other religious traditions in the world and so, beyond understanding for the minds stuck in their respective faiths. Swami Vivekananda's charge on Buddhism that he was not understood properly by his disciples is born out of this kind of misunderstanding and inability of having Buddhist approach to understand Buddhism. Lal Mani Joshi's comment is right when he questioned, "If the disciples of the Great Master did not understand His teachings properly, then who else understood them?" and commented: "It is a very radical and ridiculous proposition indeed to say that Anand, Sariputta, Mahakasyapa, Nagasena, Nagarjuna Buddhaghosa, Vasubandhu, Dharmakirti, Shantideva and Shantarakshita and others of their tradition misunderstood and misinterpreted the teachings of the Buddha, and that modern Hindus have found out the correct and real meaning of the Buddha's word. In order to vindicate the theory of Vedic-Brahamanic origin of Buddhism one has to go to the extent of falsifying the cardinal principles of classical Buddhism. We cannot accept such a theory."

The Buddha did not accept the claim of the Brahmins being equal to Sramanas. He has categorically refuted the claim of a born brahmin and stated that the Buddha, the Arhant, the Sugata are only to be called Brahmins. It was the Emperor Ashoka, maybe for political reasons, who gave equal treatment to the born Brahmins and the Buddhist Sramans. Dr. Ambedkar has held King Ashoka guilty of this mistake.

There are still many misunderstandings about Buddhism born out of Vedic-Brahmanic school of origin of Buddhism. But this is not the place to deal with those subjects. The readers are advised to read Lal Mani Joshi's *Discerning the Buddha* (Delhi, 1983).

It is also worth mentioning here that the respected Goenka Guruji, in his meeting with the leaders of Vishva Hindu Parishad and Shankaracharya, revealing the fallacy of the Buddha as an Avatar or incarnation of Vishnu and Sramanic and Brahmanic traditions being one and the same Vedic tradition, said it was accepted by the Shankaracharya and jointly declared that the Buddha was not an Avatara of Vishnu and the Sramanic tradition was different and distinct from that of Brahmanic tradition. Let us hope that it will ultimately put an end to all confusion born out of the theory of Vedic-Brahmanic origin of Buddhism.

For the ultimate good of the mankind or in the words of the Buddha, 'for the welfare and happiness of the many', the unsullied Dhamma of the Buddha has to be revived in India.

This was the task Dr. Ambedkar who inaugurated and wanted to dedicate his life for its propagation. A departure from it in any form or figure is not only an act of betrayal but rather an act of sabotage; it's an act not only of disloyalty to him, but also the damnation of his mission for humanity, in so far as deprival of people from its ultimate goodness is concerned. Therefore, the responsibility of this betrayal does not rest only with the followers and admirers of Dr. Ambedkar, but also applies to all Indians who knowingly or unknowingly refused to understand Dr. Ambedkar and his revival of Buddhism. Dr Ambedkar did care for one and all; but we Indians really care for none! He gave us the most precious gift of the Buddha's Dhamma, not something of his own creation. The habitual energy of caste consciousness compels a majority of Indian minds to look down upon Dr. Ambedkar because he was untouchable. But to look down upon Buddhism that he gave is travesty of human status itself. It's time to make amends. The author of this book has done a great service to Indian people by writing this book. In conclusion, I would like to say, let all Indians join in chorus with Prof. Rhys David (Narada, pp.291-2) saying: "Buddhist or no Buddhist, I have examined every one of the great religious systems of the world, and in none of those have I found anything to surpass in beauty and comprehensiveness the Noble Eightfold Path of the Buddha. I am content to shape my life according to that path."

Bhadant Vimalakitti Gunasiri

Founder Chairman/Director, Mahanag Sakyamuni Vijjasan, An International School of Buddhist Studies & Research, and *The Bodhisatva Babasaheb Ambedkar Buddhist Academy, Nagpur*

Acknowledgements

I was for quite some time thinking of bringing out a book showing how Dr. Babasaheb Ambedkar has been betrayed by his followers and admirers. But I found myself in the dilemma of Hamlet—whether to do it or not to do it.

I shared my views with my well wisher Dr. J.S. Sardar, who has unflinching faith in Dr. Ambedkar. He encouraged me to bring out the book, may what come. He introduced me to the Venerable Vimalakitti Gunasiri at Aurangabad, who is an ardent admirer and supporter of Dr. Ambedkar. In the very first meeting, we found ourselves, by and large, on the same wavelength. Subsequently, I had a long sitting with him on 26 June 2010 in Mumbai. I showed him the three chapters I had already prepared. After going through them said what I have written is absolutely true. This opinion of his led me to make up my mind to go ahead.

I sincerely thank Dr. J.S. Sardar and Ven. Vimalakitti Gunasiri for their encouragement.

I discussed the entire outline of the book with my philosopher and guide, Hon'ble Justice Chandrashekhar Dharmadhikari. He said that there is a need to show the true state of affairs. But the approach should be positive to motivate the Ambedkarites to carry his legacy in the right spirit and right direction. He further said that Dr. Ambedkar has not been understood as he was. His advice was before me as a beacon light. The readers will find the reflection of his advice in the book. I am indebted to Justice Dharmadhikari not only for his guidance and advice, but also for so kindly writing the 'Foreword' which is thought-provoking and will help in understanding Dr. Ambedkar and his legacy.

I am beholden to Shri Dhirubhai Mehta, who is wholeheartedly with me in my Gandhian activities and book-writing projects. He is a true Gandhian. At the same time he holds Dr. Babasaheb Ambedkar very high in his esteem. The deserving and promising scheduled castes students have preferential treatment in his National Medical College, Wardha and other institutions and organizations in which he has a decisive voice.

Shri Dhirubhai is a person who has to race against time, he being the President of the Kasturba Gandhi National Memorial Trust, Kasturba Gandhi National Medical College, Wardha, a Trustee of Gujarat Vidyapeeth, Ahemadabad and now a Trustee of Gandhi Smarak Nidhi, Delhi. But whenever I seek his appointment, he says that he has always time for me. It is his greatness and goodness.

Shri Ankushrao Kadam, who is Secretary of Mahatma Gandhi Mission (M.G.M), has a spontaneous 'yes' for my projects. It is certainly out of his affectionate regards for me. To be of use for good causes is in his blood. And this quality he has inherited from his mother , the late Smt. Rukhminidevi, and father the late Shri Nanasaheb Kadam, whose magnanimity of heart and mind was to the point of bankruptcy.

I have made extensive use of almost all the volumes of Dr. Babasaheb Ambedkar's *Writings & Speeches*, published by the Government of Maharashtra. I have also made use of *Gandhi and Ambedkar: A Study in Contrast* written by Rameshray Roy, published by Shipra Publications New Delhi; *Last Few Years of Dr. Ambedkar and Little Known Facets of Dr. Ambedkar* written by Nanak Chand Rattu, published by Amrit Publishing House, New Delhi and *Focus Impressions*, New Delhi respectively; *Dr. Ambedkar: Life & Mission* written by Dhananjay Keer, published by Popular Prakashan, Mumbai; *Buddhisten In Indien Heute* by Detlef Kantowsky and Jawaharlal Nehru's *Discovery of India*, published by Penguin Books. I place my sense of gratitude on record to the authors and publishers of the above books.

My granddaughters and grandsons are my strength. They willingly come forward to share my burden. The typing layout of this book have been done by my granddaughters Apurva, Nikita and Rucha. The work of printout as and when required has been done by my grandson Anurag. I have all appreciation and blessings for them. In fact, they are my tonic to keep me alive and active.

Sheshrao Chavan

Contents

1

Introduction

> The revival of Buddhism is, I repeat,
> one of the possibilities in India.
> William Hunter

Nobel Laureate Rabindranath Tagore had sent forth a call awaiting the arrival of the Buddha saying:

> Bring to this country once again
> The Blessed name,
> Which made the land of thy birth,
> Sacred to all distant lands!
> Let thy great awakening under the
> Bodhi Tree be fulfilled.
> Let open the doors that are barred,
> The resounding conch shells,
> Proclaim thy arrival at Bharat's Gate
> Let through innumerable voices,
> The gospel of an un-measureble love
> Announce thy call.

Dr. Ambedkar fulfilled the prediction of William Hunter made in 1881 and the call of Rabindranath Tagore on 14 October 1956 by embracing Buddhism himself and making over five lakhs of people from his community embrace Buddhism on the same day.

Dr. Ambedkar believed that the wave of conversion would spread, and in a period of 15 years, India would become a Buddhist country and join the Buddhist world as a first rank revivalist of Buddhism in the land of his birth.

Dr. Ambedkar also believed that if he is allowed some more years to live, he would bring the task he had undertaken to a successful end.

Wishful Thinking

To me, it appears that it was a wishful thinking of Ambedkar for these reasons: (i) He himself, while giving the reasons for the death of Buddhism in India said, Buddhism faded away in India because of the rise of Vaishnavitism and Shaivsism. Another was the Muslim invasion of India. When Allauddin marched into Bihar, he killed over 5,000 Bhikkhus. The remaining Buddhist monks fled to neighbouring countries like China, Nepal and Tibet. Efforts were subsequently made by Buddhists of India to raise another priesthood in order to revive Buddhism. But these efforts failed as by then 90 per cent Buddhists had embraced Hinduism. (ii) Answering a question why Hinduism survived in India and Buddhism died, Ambedkar said: "This religion is difficult to practice, while Hinduism is not." (iii)Ambedkar made a beginning of conversion only with Mahars with the hope that in course of time other castes and sub-castes would embrace Buddhism.

For the revival of Buddhism, the first task was to bring back the 90 per cent Bhikkhus to Buddhism. The opinion held by Ambedkar about the Bhikkhus is no secret. Precisely for the conduct of the Bhikkhus, he had initially refused to go to the refuse of the Sanghas. But this is said to be with a view to alert the Bhikkhus all over the world to come on the right path for the spread of Buddhism in India in particular and the world in general.

The second task, as proclained by Ambedkar himself, was that it was easy to follow Hinduism but difficult to follow Buddhism. The situation remains the same. How many neo-Buddhists observe the principles of Panchasheel, the eightfold-path and 22 Vows laid down by Ambedkar is a matter for introspection and research.

Ambedkar had also declared that religion should no longer be inherited from father to son like goods and chattels, but should be examined rationally by everybody before personal acceptance.

Ambedkar had said in his address in Bombay on 24 May 1956 that he ways writing a book on 'Dhamma Diksha.' Everyone would have to purchase this book and everyone would have to answer the questions given therein. Only thereafter they would get entry into Buddhism.

Ambedkar also said that he would have to undergo the ordeal of Moses of *Bible*. Moses had to work hard and undergo sufferings for the rehabilitation of the slaves in Palestine. He used to purchase slaves from Egypt and bring them to Palestine to free them from slavery. Ambedkar said that he would have to meet the fate of Moses for the revival and spread of Buddhism. This shows that Ambedkar was conscious of his task.

After the Mahaparinirvana of Ambedkar, the wave of Buddhism has not only faded but Buddhism has become synonymous with the Mahars. And this has been said by no less a person than the venerable Vimalakitti Gunasiri in his editorial and article in the April/May 2010 issue of his *Vijit Sangram* which every follower of Ambedkar must read to take a lesson.

Mahasthavir G. Pradyanand was one of those who gave Dhamma Diksha to Ambedkar. He was then 26 years old. He is today 84 years old. While speaking to *Lokmat Marathi Daily* at Nagpur on 16 October 2010 the venerable. Pradyanand said: "It pains me to say that even after 54 years of Dr. Babasaheb Ambedkar's taking Diksha, neo-Buddhists do not seem to be following the path laid down by Babasaheb. They are directionless. They have shattered the dream of Babasaheb. They are seen busy in the mad race for power and pelf."

Shri Namdev Dhasal, the founder of Dalit Panther, and a dispassionate virulent critic, says: "Babasaheb made 22 vows mandatory for his followers, but these vows are being thrown to the wind by his followers. All his light and heavy weight Buddhists have not adopted the teachings and preachings of Buddhism as interpreted by Babasaheb Ambedkar. They have confined Buddhism to one caste of the untouchables. They do not understand the difference between Hinayana and Mahayana. As a result the scheduled castes have gone back to pavilion and are worshipping Hindu gods, goddesses and deities. They are also continuing to believe in blind faith. Not only this, but the so-called Buddhist monks bring Buddha's idols in meditation from countries like Japan, Combodia and Thailand and install them in the Pagoda-type Viharas constructed by them, and are making money. The true followers of Ambedkar have given up fighting for the spread of real Buddhism." (*Lokmat*, 17th October 2010.)

Ambedkar in his Diksha address explicitly said: "Mahars should do nothing that will bring a bad name. You must lead such a life that you may command respect. Do not think that this religion is like the dog-collar tied round your neck." It may be recollected what Ambedkar told his followers: "So far as Buddhism is concerned this country of ours has become a desert. Now it has fallen on you that you should endeavour to follow this religion sincerely and always keep in view the position it had once attained. If you do not do so, people will laugh at this conversion."

The converted Buddhists need to go for an introspection to see how far they have come up to the expectations of Dr. Ambedkar. And wake up from their slumber to act upon Ambedkar's command: "Every one of you has to take Diksha. Organize a huge machinery for the propagation of Dhamma. Every Buddhist has the right to initiate others. Go forth with the message of the Buddha. Go forth to liberate people."

They must also bear in mind what Appasaheb Pant, in his capacity as the High Commissioner of India to United Kingdom, said: "Babasaheb Ambedkar gave a call not only to those downtrodden and oppressed but to all Indians to break down their shackles and bonds by seeing the truth in the Buddhist way of life and creating a new society of harmony and happiness around them."

For this, the converted Buddhists will have to stop swimming in the pond and start swimming in the ocean to bring people from all the strata of society into the Buddhist fold. The failure of converted Buddhists, if continued, will prove what Jawaharlal Nehru said in his *Discovery of India.* "It must be remembered that Hinduism was at no time wholly displaced by Buddhism. Even when Buddhism was at its height in India, Hinduism was widely prevalent."

Vimalakitti Gunasiri, however, does not agree with Jawaharlal Nehru. According to him Buddhism existed many years before the Vedic period. In its known history, Buddhism did see its decline at times, but it was mainly for two reasons: (i) Deliberate efforts were made to suppress it through methods of coercion by the forces which were afraid that Buddhism would drive out Hinduism. (ii) There was no organized set-up for the spread and upkeep of Buddhism on the lines of Christianity and Islam.

He further says that in one of the International Buddhist Conferences, he himself had raised his voice and said that the organizations with adequate funds on the lines of Christianity and Islam should be evolved. But his voice went into deaf ears.

I am inclined to agree with him. The Buddhist organizations, all over the world, and more particularly in India, will have to give serious thought to strengthen and expand their organizations by raising ample funds to launch a drive and sustain it to achieve the goal. This is absolutely necessary in India in view of the changed attitude of the people to look at Buddhism. This task is very arduous, but not impossible. The converted Buddhists will have to work hand in hand burying their internal differences whatsoever and mobilize forces to revive Buddhism as envisaged by Ambedkar.

The teachings of Buddha will alone bring India out of the grip of the three Ms, i.e., Money power, Muscle power and Mafia power. The greed, hatred and attachment are at the root of three Ms. People, in general, are tired of the three Ms, and if a methodical massive drive is launched by Buddhist organizations, there may be an overwhelming response from the people.

I visited Thailand in 2004, where Buddhism is still a dominant faith. I saw there temples and monasteries. I met monks and laymen. Despite Buddha's teachings and warnings, they worship him as God. Many monks, although themselves ignorant persons, demand obeisance from the innocent people. I witnessed more or less the same in America during my visits there. When I brought this to the notice of Shri. Vimalakitti, he said: "People look at Buddha as *Devas* as *Sathaa, Deva-Manu-Sassanan* and therefore they worship him as the Lord of Gods."

In India the monasteries have been made the places of worship of Buddha with his idol installed in them. This makes me think whether his followers are really following him as he thought and taught, or are using him for their designs.

The same thing is being done with regard to Dr. Ambedkar, who himself said that he believed neither in God nor in soul, and yet he is worshipped as God.

I honestly feel that the converted Buddhists should not look at Ambedkar as God, but follow him. What he said was that Buddha is thousand times better than us. Otherwise the Buddhists may do great disservice to the glory of Ambedkar, and also to the revival and spread of Buddhism in India.

Educate, Agitate and Organize

This was the mantra given by Dr. Ambedkar to his brethren to arouse their conscious to free themselves from the age-old tyranny of Hindus. He firmly believed that education could not only new bring consciousness among the downtrodden but also impel them towards a praxis of self-liberation. While welcoming Dr. Rajendra Prasad, the first President of free India, in his Milind Mahavidyalaya at Aurangabad on 1 September 1951, Dr. Ambedkar said:

> Coming as I do from the lowest order of the Hindu society, I know what is the value of education. The problem of raising the lower order in India is not of feeding them, clothing them, but the problem is to remove from them the inferiority complex which has stunted their growth and made them slaves to others, to create in them the consciousness of the significance of their lives for themselves and for the country, of which they have been cruelly robbed of the existing social order. Nothing can achieve this purpose except the spread of higher education.

He established the People's Education Society in 1945 and started colleges under it to achieve the purpose.

He left the People's Education Society on a sound foundation to achieve the purpose but those on whom the mantle fell after him to develop the colleges shattered the dream his. At the fag end of his life, he was so much disillusioned that he said: "I am disappointed with the educated men of my community; I have now pinned hopes on illiterates."

On the strength of his education, Ambedkar could have obtained the highest office in India. When he returned home after completing his education in America and Europe, he was offered the post of District Judge. He was promised to be elevated to the High Court within three subsequent years. He declined the offer saying that he did not want those alluring ties. He feared that after getting into government service, he would not be able to serve his people. Keeping this in view, he kept himself away from government service.

He again said: "From my early childhood I have dedicated myself to the upliftment of the scheduled castes among whom I was born. It is not that there were no temptations in my way. If I had considered my own interest, I could have been anything I wanted to be, and if I had joined the Congress, I would have reached the highest place in that organization. But as I said, I had dedicated myself to the upliftment of the scheduled castes and I have followed the adage which says that it is better to be narrow-minded if you wish to be enthusiastic about the cause which you wish to accomplish. You can, therefore, well imagine what pain it has caused me to see that the cause of the scheduled castes has been relegated to the limbo of nothing." (*Dr. Babasahed Ambedkar- Writings & Speeches* Vol. 14, p.1321)

Dr. Ambedkar left for the Divine Abode with this agony in his heart.

The Dream Remained a Dream

Ambedkar fundamentally opposed the political domination of one community over the other. He said that in a caste-ridden society like India having numerical domination of upper caste Hindus, the adult franchise would automatically empower this communal majority to capture state machinery. He, however, said that the adult franchise can also be used as a device to check the communal majority and to acquire political power by the scheduled castes, scheduled tribes and backward classes. He further said that the Constitution of India has made the deprived classes virtually the masters as they form the majority of the population of the country and there is no reason why they should not rule the country. All that is necessary is to organize a third force.

With this view in mind he floated the idea of forming the Republican Party of India. He argued: "It is only through this force that scheduled castes and deprived classes will be able to acquire effective bargaining power, especially when there is no political party with an absolute majority." In such a situation, his calculations were that other political parties would rise to their feet and beg for their support. Thus, they would hold the balance of power and dictate their terms to these political parties.

The Republican Party of India did come into existence in 1957, but after the sad demise of Ambedkar with a house divided. As a result the leaders of the Republican Party of India, instead of bringing the Hindu dominant parties to their feet, were seen crawling it the feet of the leaders of this Congress or that Congress for crumbs of pelf and power. And now leaders like Ramdas Athawale are on the verge of joining hands with Shivsena supremo Balasaheb Thakre with the hope that Shiv-shakti and Bhim-shakti would drive the Congress out of power.

Kanshiram could build the Bahujan Samaj Party to become a ruling party in UP. This is because he could unite 600 castes as claimed by himself in his speech at the first convention of

Dalits held at Kuala Lumpur in Malasiya. Mayavati has continued to carry the legacy of her mentor.

The leadership that emerged to fill Ambedkar's place was not only of lesser calibre and stature, but it also lacked the agility that Ambedkar displayed in swiftly changing his position in a changed political situation. This was his dynamism, but it proved to be a problem for the leadership that came after him as it lacked his qualities. This resulted in split after split and fractions of the dalit movement, each fraction representing entirely a different social base and adopting different political strategies.

In Maharashtra, the Republican Party of India was confined mainly to the Mahars, with scanty exceptions, who embraced Buddhism. This narrowed down the support base of the Republican Party of India at the cost of decreasing the number of Ambedkar's followers in other states of India. There is hardly any hope that wisdom will dawn on the leaders of the Republican Party of India to bring others into its fold those who believed in Ambedkar's principles of liberty, equality and fraternity.

Ramashray Roy in his book *Gandhi and Ambedkar—A Study in Contrast* at page 187 says: "..Every effort to unite the Dalits and their different constituents only created new cracks in the ranks of Dalits and the jealousy fed upon the lust for power among the Dalit leaders and aspirants to leadership positions in a situation where the position vacated by the death of Ambedkar attracted many ambitious aspirants to occupy the top position that the party could offer. However, none of them was capable enough to keep together the flock tended so laboriously by Ambedkar."

Ambedkar said: "I have not been able to fulfil my life's ambition to see my people a governing class in my lifetime sharing the political power."

This is another pinch which must be troubling Dr. Ambedkar's soul although he did not believe in the concept of a soul.

Tough Bargainer

Dr. Ambedkar hated the caste system, untouchability and the inequalities of the old Indian society with a glowing, incandescent hatred. He fought those social ills and injustices ruthlessly and with unmatched political skill. But that did not prevent him from remaining a staunch Indian nationalist. What he was trying was to bargain, and he was a tough bargainer, with the British and Indian leaders for the maximum he could get for his community in terms of political safeguards. That was his intention and not to compromise on Indian independence.

Dr. Ambedkar had taken the vow: "If I fail to do away with the abominable thralldom and inhuman injustice under which the class, into which I was born has been groaning, I will put to an end myself with a bullet." The constitution abolished untouchability and this vow was fulfilled.

Patriot of Sterling Qualities

There are some people who question the patriotism of Dr. Ambedkar. For them, I quote what he said in 1930: "To say that this country is divided by castes and creeds and that it cannot be one united self-governing community unless adequate safeguards for protection of minorities are made as part of the Constitution is a position to which there can be no objection; but the minorities must bear in mind that although we are today driven by and atomized by caste, our ideal is a united India. That being so, it follows that every minority in formulating the safeguards it needs must take care that they will not be incompatible with realization of this great ideal."

Speaking in the Bombay Legislative Assembly on 4 April 1938 on the Bill for the creation of a separate Karnataka Province Ambedkar said: "...I do not like what some people say, that we are Indians first and Hindus afterwards or Muslims afterwards. I am not satisfied with that, I frankly say that I am not satisfied with that. I do not want that our loyalty as Indians should be in the slightest way affected by only competitive loyalty. Whether that loyalty arises out of our religion, out of our culture or out of a language, I want all people to be Indians first, Indians last and nothing else but Indians."

Again speaking at a meeting in Bombay on 10 January 1950, Dr. Ambedkar exhorted his community to think not merely of itself, but also of the country as a whole. He said: "India was enslaved by the Muslims and the British, but today we are free and we should exert ourselves to ensure that history does not repeat itself." He further said: "We were called the stooges of the British and the Muslims but we had to bargain with the former because we were not free and were compelled to safeguard our own interests."

Dr. Ambedkar's speeches in the Constituent Assembly on 4 November 1948, 25 and 26 November 1949 speak for his deep concern for India and his sterling patriotism.

To say that Ambedkar was not patriotic is far from the truth and without foundation.

Irony of Fate

Ambedkar condemned Manu, but he was hailed as a Modern Manu for drafting the Constitution. He hated hero-worship for he considered it a sure road to degradation, while his followers consider hero-worship as a sure road to climb up. He did not believe in God, whereas his community worships him as God. Corruption was anathema to him, while it is a gospel for his followers to achieve pelf and power. Educational institutions were centres of learning for Ambedkar, but they are centres of money making for his followers. His first and last priority was interests of the scheduled castes, whereas his followers' first and last priority is their own welfare.

I am reminded of what George Bernard Shaw said and I quote: "Not knowing how to punish great men for their greatness, fate punishes them by giving disciples."

Justice Chandrashekhar Dharmadhikari has expressed it succinctly: "Disciples have the right to perform the last rites of their Gurus, but they seldom become their successors. Instead of raising themselves to the level of their Gurus, they bring down their Gurus to their level."

Hindu Code Bill

The Hindu Code Bill was a monumental work of Dr. Ambedkar. But I feel he made haste in tendering his resignation as Law Minister. Hindu Code Bill seems to be the apparent reason. But there seems to be other deep reasons and he was waiting for an opportunity.

Dr. Ambedkar was shrewd enough to continue as Law Minister until the adoption of the Draft Constitution by the Constituent Assembly because he knew that by remaining in the Constituent Assembly, he would be able to protect the interests of his community in particular, and the interests of India in general.

Dr. Ambedkar was probably feeling humiliated and isolated in the Cabinet which is evident from what he said in his statement of resignation which is at Annexure I.

Ambedkar was not satisfied with the law portfolio given to him by Nehru. He said: "As a result of my being a member of Viceroy's Council, I knew the Law Ministry to be administratively of no importance. It gave no opportunity for shaping the policy of the Government of India. We used to call it an empty soap-box only good for old lawyers to play with. When the Prime Minister made me the offer, I told him that besides being a lawyer by my education and experience, I was competent to run any administrative department, and that in the old Viceroy's Executive Council I held two administrative portfolios, that of Labour and C.P.W.D., where a great deal of planning projects were dealt with by me and would like to have some administrative portfolio. The Prime Minister agreed and said he would give me in addition to Law the Planning Department which, he said, was intending to create. Unfortunately the Planning Department came very late in the day and when it did come I was left out. During my time, there have been many transfers of portfolios from one Minister to another. I thought I might be considered for any one of them. But I have always been left out of consideration. Many Ministers have been given two or three portfolios so that they have been overburdened. Others like me have been wanting more work. I have not even been considered for holding a portfolio temporarily when a Minister in charge has gone abroad for a few days. It is difficult to understand what principle is underlying the distribution of Government work among Ministers which the Prime Minister follows. Is it capacity? Is it trust? Is it friendship? Is it pliability? I was not even appointed to be a member of main the Committees of the Cabinet such as the Foreign Affairs Committee or the Defence Committee. When the Economic Affairs Committee was formed, I expected, in view of the fact that I was primarily a student of Economics and Finance, to be appointed to this Committee. But I was left out. I was appointed to it by the Cabinet, when the Prime Minister had gone to England. But when he returned, in one of his many essays in the reconstruction of the Cabinet, he left me out. In a subsequent reconstruction my name was added to the committee, but that was as a result of my protest."

The press of those days held Ambedkar equally responsible for his debacle which can be seen from the following comments.

"Ambedkar is the sad example of a man with a genius but no judgement. In British Rule, he flaunted his untouchability like a proud emblem. But the guilt was wearing thin. He should never have resigned from the central cabinet. It was a miscalculation which cost him and his community dear."

"Had he stayed on as Law Minister, he would have done both his community and country a service."

"The Congress never forgot the reasons given by him for his resignation. In the general election of 1952, it opposed tooth and nail Ambedkar in a Bombay Constituency successfully. The Congress again frustrated his efforts to secure a seat in Parliament. Ambedkar became increasingly bitter and lavished even harsher criticism on the Government, which made him nearly a roaring lion."

The life of Dr. Ambedkar provides an example as well as an inspiration to all those who constitute the have-nots and the downtrodden and tell them that no bar based on class, caste, riches or privileges can come in the way of an individual who is determined to go up. His was in defiance of the arrogance of those who held that individual elevation was the monopoly of the privileged few.

Prof. J. Raghavendra, in his Dr. B.R. Ambedkar Memorial lecture series on 6 December 1988 at Hyderabad said: "Bodhisatva Bharat Ratna Dr. Babasaheb Ambedkar was one of those wretched of the earth, the lowliest and the lost of the Indian soil, who by sheer articulation of his genius and prodigious industry shot into the political horizon as a spectacular leader and an outstanding intellectual. He is to be reckoned with not only as a political emancipator, economist, historian and an extraordinary jurist, but a great savant and educationist too. The spectrum of his ideas or actions had not only influenced the process of emancipation of scheduled castes but many others too."

Pandit Jawaharlal Nehru on the sad demise of Ambedkar said in Parliament on 6 December 1956:

"Dr. Ambedkar for many, many years had been a controversial figure in Indian public affairs, but there can be no doubt about his outstanding quality, his scholarship, and the intensity with which he pursued his convictions, sometimes rather than with greater intensity than perhaps required by the particular subject, which sometimes reacted in a contrary way. But he was the symbol of that intense feeling which we must always remember, the intense feeling of the suppressed classes in India who have suffered for ages past under our previous social systems, and it is as well that we recognize this burden that all of us should carry and should always remember. It may be that some of us thought, as I have just said, that he overdid the expression of that feeling, but I do not think that, apart from the manner of utterance or language, anybody should challenge the rightness of the intensity of his feeling in that manner which should be felt by all of us and perhaps even more so by those who have not in themselves or in their groups or classes had to suffer from that. He was that. Therefore he became this symbol. But we in Parliament remember him for many other things and more particularly for the very prominent part he played in the making of our Constitution, and perhaps that fact will be remembered even longer than his other activities."

Shri Kamalkishore Kadam, in his capacity as the Education Minister of Maharashtra State, in his 'Preface' to the second edition of volume one of *Dr Babasaheb Ambedkar: Writings and Speeches* says and rightly says: *'The Writings and Speeches of*

Dr. Ambedkar show what values Indians should develop and how they should modernize their social and political institutions. They provide the rich source of the civilizing influences in our society. The range of his topics, the worth of his vision, the depth of his analysis, the rationality of his outlook and the essential humanity of his suggestions for action evoke ready responses. Such was Dr. Ambedkar – a man whose talents, acquirements and virtues were so extraordinary that the more his character is considered, the more he will be regarded by the present age and by posterity with admiration and reverence."

I conclude my preface by an urge that let Dr. Ambedkar's life be a perennial source of inspiration not only to those who are deprived, disadvantaged, humble and meek, but also to all those who have a dream to see India as a strong nation in the twenty-first century.

2

Born a Hindu—Will Not Die a Hindu

True to his declaration at Yeola on 13 October 1935, that he was born a Hindu, but he will not die as a Hindu, Ambedkar renounced Hinduism and embraced Buddhism on 14 October 1956 at a mammoth gathering in Nagpur.

This day was chosen as it was the auspicious day of Dhamma Vijaya, the day on which Ashoka the Great had embraced Buddhism in 262 BC and had declared that henceforth, he would conquer the people by love and persuasion instead of by force.

Ashoka, who was stigmatized as wicked owing to his ruthlessness in expanding his empire, became Dharmashoka or Ashoka the Righteous, and changed his career to such an extent that today amidst the tens of thousands of names of monarchs that crowd the columns of history, their majesties and graciousness and serenities and royal highneses and the like, the name of Ashoka shines almost alone, a star.

It was the 'Nagas' who spread the religion of Buddha throughout the world. These people were predominantly the inhabitants of Nagpur. Through the soil of this city, there flowed a river named 'Nag.' It appears that the Nagas lived on the banks of this river. This is mainly the reason why Ambedkar selected Nagpur for his conversion to Buddhism.

Ambedkar had invited Chandramuni Maha Thera of Kushinara to initiate him into Buddhism. "It is our great wish," he wrote to Chandramuni, "that you should officiate at the ceremony. You being the oldest monk in India, we think it would be appropriate to have the ceremony performed by you."

Maha Thera Chandramuni and his four saffron-robed Bhikkhus administered in Pali to Ambedkar and his wife, the three 'Sarans' under Buddha, Dhamma and Sangha and 'Panchsheel' of five precepts of abstention from killing, stealing, telling lies, wrongful sex life and drink. They repeated the Pali mantras in Marathi. Then they bowed down thrice with clasped hands before the Buddha statuettes, and offerings of white lotuses before it. With this Ambedkar's entry into Buddhistic fold was announced.

Thereafter, Ambedkar was profoundly garlanded by D. Valisinha, General Secretary of the Maha Bodhi Society of India.

Ambedkar then declared: "By discarding my ancient religion which stood for inequality and oppression, today I am reborn. I am no more a devotee of any Hindu god or goddess. I will strictly follow the eightfold path of Buddha. Buddhism is a true religion and I will lead a life guided by the three principles of knowledge, right path and compassion."

Now a Buddhist, Ambedkar called upon those who wanted to embrace Buddhism to stand up. The entire gathering rose up, and he administered the three refuges and five precepts and different pledges to the vast gathering, which was said to be over five lakhs.

The next day, on 15 October, Ambedkar initiated another vast crowed of his followers into Buddhism at the same place. Thereafter, he delivered his speech. Explaining the reasons for his renouncing Hinduism and embracing Buddhism, He said:

"For a man it is his birthright to lead an honourable life. To achieve this aim we must do our utmost. We are prepared to make the greatest sacrifice for achieving this. We are struggling for human dignity which the Hindus had hitherto denied to us. We want to make our life as full and wholesome as possible.

"There are many things we may have to sacrifice on our embracing Buddhism. So far as the concessions, such as reservations etc. are concerned, let me assure you they shall not be lost. After the ceremony, the first problem that I shall devote my attention would be the problem of these concessions.

"Those who are capable of achieving the rights have the strength and the capacity to retain them too. We shall have to do a great deal for the progress of this movement. Many problems will crop up after the acceptance of Buddhism. How shall we face the situation? How shall we brave the many difficulties that may arise? I have sufficient strength and material in hand to grapple with the problems. I fought for these rights and secured them for you. I assure you, I will get them again for you. Of course, what may happen after my death, I cannot say.

"Have confidence in me and the words I am uttering. There is absolutely no truth in the words of our opponents. I say unto you, pay no heed to their words.

"The question of our conversion is being discussed everywhere but I am surprised to see that nobody has asked me the reason why of all the religions I have chosen the religion of Buddha. In any movement of conversion this is a significant question to be asked. At the time of embracing a religion one should ask oneself these questions, namely:

"1. Which religion should be adopted?

"2. How it should be adopted?

"Unfortunately, Hinduism which is founded on the ideologies of inequality and injustice leaves no room for the development of enthusiasm. So long as the untouchables continue to slave under the yoke of Hinduism, a diabolical creed they can have no hope, no inspiration, no enthusiasm for better life. They might produce no more than a few hundred clerks poor clerks who will do nothing except fill their bellies. What else can they do? Then we shall need super clerks to protect them from injustices and various kinds of atrocities. The common masses of the untouchables will not gain anything. The scheduled castes can never feel enthusiastic about and derive inspiration from the ideologies prevailing in Hinduism.

"Besides the lack of congenial atmosphere there is also lack of equality among Hindus.

"The religion and this social order has ruined us. But this is not going to stop here. This would ruin the Hindus themselves and ultimately India.

"I do not accuse the Hindu religion in vain. The religion cannot save anybody. It has no life left in it.

"Why has our country lost her freedom time and again? Why have we been subjected to foreign domination so often?

It is because this country as a whole never stood against the enemy. It was always a small section of the society, and whoever overpowered it became the victor. This is mainly due to the pernicious caste system of the Hindus.

"Hinduism cannot save anybody. There is no salvation for anybody in Hinduism. According to the tenets of Hinduism only the so-called higher castes have benefited. There is no exaggeration in my statement. What have the Shudras and Untouchables gained?

"As soon as the wife of a Brahmin conceives, she thinks of the High Court, whether any post of a Judge has fallen vacant, but when our woman becomes pregnant, she cannot think of anything better than a sweeper's post under the municipal committee.

"This deplorable situation exists only because Hinduism has inculcated this kind of ambition in the former and the degradation in the latter. No change in our status can be expected if we continue to be slaves of Hinduism. If we have any hope it is by renouncing Hinduism and following the path of the Buddha. Let us now consider the principles of Buddhism.

"The fundamental principle of Buddhism is equality. Of all the Bhikkhus who joined the Order in the time of Lord Buddha about 75 per cent of the Bhikkhus belonged to the Brahmin caste and the remaining 25 per cent were Shudras. Even then Buddhism was called the religion of the Shudras.

"The Bhikkhus, who belong to different castes and have come from the various lands just as the great rivers when they have fallen into the great ocean, lose their identity. Just so O' brethren, do these four castes, Kshatriyas, Brahmins, Vaishyas, Shudras when they begin to follow the doctrine and discipline as propounded by the Tathagatha, they renounced different names of castes and rank and became members of one and the same society. These are the words of Buddha...

"There was only one man who raised his voice against the separatism and untouchability and that was Lord Buddha.

"In the beginning Lord Buddha got only ten or twelve Bhikkhus. Out of these nine or ten were Shudras. This is evident from the autobiographical 'gathas' of the Bhikkus entitled as 'Theragatha' and 'Therigatha.' Their writings bear testimony to the fact that Buddhism is the only religion which does not recognize caste and afford full scope for progress.

"My political opponents who observed my political activities very keenly say that I am a cunning fox. They say that I want to extract as many concessions for the scheduled castes as it is possible to get. On the other hand, there are some who wonder as to why I have taken so long to take a decision in regard to the change of religion. What have you been doing all these years, they ask. The only reply I can give is this that the question of religion is the most difficult and a very serious question. It is a matter of enormous responsibility, really, to educate the people in regard to the merits of this religion and to inculcate in the people the habit of behaving according to the principles of 'Dhamma'. There is no other person who had to shoulder so grave a responsibility, nor do I think anybody will be called upon to shoulder such a heavy responsibility in future. If I am allowed some more years to live, I shall bring the task that I have undertaken today, to a successful end.

"Some people will naturally ask this question, what will the untouchables gain by embracing Buddhism? Suffice to say that it is a worthless question. Is religion necessary for the well-to-do? No, perhaps not.

"Those who are holding high positions in life have nice bungalows to live in, money to buy all comforts of life and servants to attend on them, and perhaps, have little use for religion.

"This reminds me of my German professor Winternitz.

The Watergang Rabelan Depth was the book which he recommended and by which I was much inspired. It is, he said: 'Only the poor who need religion. Hope is the spring of action in life. Religion affords this hope. Therefore, mankind finds solace in the religion, that is why the poor cling to religion.'

"When Christianity made its way into Europe, the situation in and around Rome was appalling. People did not get enough food to fill their bellies; they lived in abject poverty. But do you know, who were the people who extended a sympathetic response to the call of Christianity when it penetrated into Rome? Not those who were convinced of its spirituality but those miserable poor and oppressed people who were served a meal free of cost—people who worked as slaves and served for their Roman masters. The poor and the oppressed became converts to Christianity. Mr. Gibbon, the renowned historian and the author of *The Rise and Fall of the Roman Empires* scornfully branded Christianity as a religion of the poor and the beggars. Mr. Gibbon is not alive today. He would have been shocked to see the whole of Europe engulfed by Christianity.

"Some people, here in India, will no doubt say that this Buddhism is the religion of the untouchables. They will malign and pass disparaging remarks. Brahmins in their time did not spare even Bhagwan Buddha. Irreverently they addressed him as 'O Gautama' or, 'Bho Gautama'. They wanted to show disrespect towards him. They wanted to insult him.

"In spite of all the vilifications and the abuses showered on this religion, Buddhism has cultivated better acquaintances in Europe and America than Hinduism. You will be surprised to know that if the images of Rama, Krishna, Shankara or any other Hindu deity are kept for sale or export, nobody would care to buy them. Instead, if the images of Buddha are kept in the morning for sale none will be found in the evening.

"Inside India much has been done to publicise Hinduism. It is time that they went outside and told the world of what they have. If there is any name which is known outside India, which is popular and revered, it is not the name of Rama or Krishna, but it is the name of Buddha. Nobody knows Rama or Krishna outside India. There is no reason why this religion of ours should not spread throughout the world. Much will depend on how we live it.

"We shall go ahead undauntedly on the path we have chosen. We have found a new way to life and we shall follow it. This path leads to progress.

"In fact, this is not something new nor have we imported it from outside. Buddhism is the religion of this country. It is more than 2,000 years old. I feel sorry that I did not embrace this religion earlier. The teachings of the Buddha are eternal but even then Buddha did not proclaim them to be infallible.

The religion of Buddha has the capacity to change according to times, a quality which no other religion can claim to have.

"You must bear in mind the following four facts in respect of Buddhism. You must never think that the teachings of the Buddhism are of temporary value and are not likely to last longer. Even after a lapse of 2,500 years the world respects the teachings of the Buddha. There are as many as 2,000 institutions of the followers of Buddhism in the United States of America. In England a Buddha temple has been built at a cost of Rs. 300,000. There are some 3,000 or 4,000 institutions founded in the name of Buddha in Germany.

"The principles and teachings of Bhagwan Buddha are eternal, but in spite of this fact Buddha did not claim any status for himself, nor did he claim the principles to be infallible. He never claimed divinity for himself or for his religion. Buddha did not say that he was the son of God or the last Prophet messenger of God. On the contrary he said: 'My father and my mother are ordinary mortals.'

"Now, what is the basis of Buddhism? If you study carefully, you will see that Buddhism is based on reasons. There is an element of flexibility inherent in it which is not to be found in any other religion.

"Only those people should embrace this religion, who earnestly believe in it. If they do not believe in it or it does not appeal to them, they should not embrace it. For, such high principles are not to be found in any other religion. There is a world of difference between this religion and any other religion of the world. The main principles of Buddhism form no part of theistic religion. According to other religions God created the world, this earth and thereafter he created heaven, air, moon and other planets. That means he had created, also the stone in the bladder. God has done all that was required to be done and now there remains nothing for us to do. All that we are required to do is, just to sing the praises of Almighty God. This does not appeal to the rational man today.

"Buddhism denies the existence of God and soul. The real basis of Buddhism is the rational way to eradicate suffering. 'There is,' Buddha said, 'suffering in the world—suffering wide-spread.' Ninety per cent people are afflicted with suffering or misery of some kind or the other. The main object of Buddhism is to emancipate the suffering humanity. The question arises, then what is the use of *Das Kapital?* I believe that Karl Marx was far behind Buddha, for he did not say anything that had not been brought to light by Buddha himself, some 2,400 years before Marx was born.

"Some people say that Buddhism is on its deathbed or practically dead. If it is so, it is our duty to raise it to a better status. We should act in a manner so as to enthuse and inspire respect, among other people. We may have a garden or a temple and arrange for discourses there.

"I will do my best by writing books or by removing your doubts. All I wish today is that you should have faith in me and follow me. The trust you repose in me will not be used for personal gain and I shall endeavour to satisfy all your doubts.

"A great responsibility has fallen on your shoulders too. Mahars should do nothing that will bring a bad name. You must lead such a life that you may command respect. Do not think that this religion is like the dog-collar tied round your neck.

"So far as Buddhism is concerned this country of ours has become a desert. Now it has fallen on you that you should endeavour to follow this religion sincerely and always keep in view the position it had once attained. If you do not do so, people will laugh at this conversion.

"This religion can serve not only this country but the whole world. At this juncture in the world affairs, Buddhism is indispensable for world peace. You must pledge today that you, the followers of Buddha, will not only work to liberate yourself, but will try to elevate your country and the world in general.

"I am reported to be against peace. This is not correct. I am for peace, but the peace, which is based on justice, not the peace of a graveyard. So long as justice is not respected in the world there cannot be any peace. Buddhism and Buddhism alone can save the world.

"This task you have taken in hand is of immense responsibility. You have to labour hard. This thing you will have to bear in mind. Hitherto most of us have been interested only in bread and butter. Do not be self-centred! Do not be selfish in your outlook.

"We need money for the propagation of this great religion. I have no mind to ask for any monetary help from any foreign country.

"You must resolve to contribute at least one-twentieth of your income for the propagation of the Dhamma. I am to carry you all with me. Bhagwan Buddha used to carry on initiation ceremony himself. When it became unmanageable for one person, he allowed that work to be shared by other competent persons among his followers. You might have heard the name of one 'Yasha'. He was the scion of a rich family. Yasha became his disciple and there were forty more men who followed him. The message given to forty Bhikkhus was: 'Go ye, O Bhikkhus, and wander forth for the gain of the many, the welfare of the many, in compassion for the world, for the good, for the gain, for the welfare of Gods and men, preach ye the Dhamma which is beneficial in the beginning, beneficial in the middle and beneficial in the end. Proclaim, O Bhikkhus, the doctrine glorious, preach ye life of holiness, perfect and pure'.

"So brothers and sisters this is my religion.

"Buddha adopted the method which was most suitable in the circumstances obtaining then, for the propagation of his religion. Accordingly, we too, should adopt the method which is most suitable in the existing circumstances. There are no Bhikkhus in this country to do his work. So, every one of you has to take 'Diksha'. A Buddhist has the right to convert others to his faith. If a disruption comes at a later stage, we must have a provision in our sleeves to meet the situation. We must organize a huge machinery for the propagation of Dhamma. Every Buddhist has the right to initiate others. I make this announcement today. Go forth with the message of the Buddha. Go forth to liberate people."

On 16 October 1956, Ambedkar attended a conversion ceremony at Chanda, where again the vast gathering of the untouchables repeated the pledges which he gave them.

Though Ambedkar's health was poor, his face was beaming with pride and joy. He was, indeed, the author of an epoch-making event. He had the divine satisfaction of having accomplished a great deed and set in motion the wheel of Dhamma once again. He had fulfilled the prediction of Sir William Hunter, who had said in 1881: "The revival of Buddhism is, I repeat, one of the possibilities in India." (*Ancient India William Hunter,* pp. 175)

Nobel Laureate Rabindranath Tagore, too, had sent forth a call, eagerly awaiting the arrival of the Buddha, saying:

> Bring to this country once again
> the blessed name,
> which made the land of thy birth
> sacred to all distant lands!
> Let thy great awakening under the
> Bodhi Tree be fulfilled;
> Let open the doors that are barred,
> and the resounding conch shell,
> Proclaim thy arrival at Bharat's
> Gate
> Let through innumerable voices, the
> gospel of an un-measurable love
> announce thy call.

To carry out the conversion in the country, Ambedkar had planned to convene a meeting of the representatives of his party, his lieutenants and important workers from each state.

The conversion was to be carried out in phases in Delhi, Mumbai, Punjab, UP and in other major cities of India. He firmly believed that the wave of conversion would spread and in a period of 15 years, India would become a Buddhist country and join the Buddhist world as a first rank revivalist of Buddhism in the land of its birth. "Brahmins," he said, "would be the last to follow and let them be the last." (Nanak Chand Rattu, *Last Few Years of Dr. Ambedkar*, pp. 108-9)

In the evening of 5 December 1956, two Jain Munis met Ambedkar and discussed with him some important questions concerning Buddhism. They were very much impressed by the scholarly study of Ambedkar of the two faiths. They left with the confession that they would like to embrace Buddhism themselves. (Nanak Chand Rattu, *Last Few Years of Dr. Ambedkar*, pp. 113)

The conversion programme at Mumbai was fixed for 16 December 1956 and Ambedkar had made the necessary travel arrangements to reach Mumbai on 14 December 1956. From Mumbai, he had proposed to go to Aurangabad. But, alas! He breathed his last on 6 December 1956 in Delhi, leaving his innumerable followers and admirers orphans.

Funeral Procession

More than 500,000 people joined the funeral procession of Ambedkar, the biggest such procession ever witnessed in the city of Mumbai. It took nearly four hours to cover a two-mile distance from Rajgriha, his residence in Dadar, to the cremation ground, near Shivaji Park.

Ambedkar had planned a massive conversion ceremony in Mumbai on 16 December 1956. To fulfil his wish, the assembled gathering insisted that they be admitted into the fold of Buddhism. Hence, an impromptu conversion ceremony was organized at the cremation ground and they were administered the Three Refuses and Five Precepts on the spot by Bhadant Anand Kausalyayan, a Punjabi monk, who stayed at Nagpur Diksha Bhoomi from 1969 to 1982 and greatly made the place a living religious centre.

3
Premature Death of Ambedkar

Ambedkar died on 6 December 1956 under a cloud of suspicion.

Second Marriage

Ambedkar's first wife, who belonged to his community, passed away on 27 May 1935. She was a woman who shared all her hardships and agony which came to the lot of her husband. In turn, Ambedkar always felt sorry and guilty for not being able to look after her, particularly during her prolonged illness.

Ambedkar remembered too often and too much his faithful wife and shed tears at times. He resolved not to go in for second marriage. "I have," he said, "lived a lonely life at least for the last 15 years. I have had no companions, but I have learned to live a happy life without asking anyone to bestow personal affection on me. My books have been my companions, they are dearer to me than wife and children." (Nanak Chand Rattu, *Last Few Years of Dr. Ambedkar*, p. 75)

Ambedkar, however, wrote to Ramakant Chitre, who was the Registrar of Siddharth College, in February 1948, that his health has suddenly deteriorated and he was facing a relapse. He passed four nights without a wink of sleep with the most excruciating pain in both the legs, and his servants had to keep awake and nurse him the whole night. "I have been examined," he further wrote, "by two most eminent doctors who say that if my condition does not improve immediately the trouble in the legs may become chronic and incurable." He revealed his mind to Chitre that he was thinking of having someone to look after him more sympathetically.

Ambedkar, having come to Mumbai, got himself admitted in the clinic of Dr. Madhav Malvankar. In his clinic there was one Dr. Miss Sharda Kabir who often attended on Ambedkar. She impressed upon him as the one who would look after him in his old age. Ambedkar was then 56 years old. She persuaded Dr. Malvankar to suggest to Ambedkar to take her to Delhi for a month to attend on him as a nurse.

Dr. Malvankar carried her wish to Ambedkar, praising the career and qualification of Sharda Kabir in high words.

Ambedkar, as a first reaction, came out heavily on Sharda Kabir for having put into the head of Dr. Malvankar the idea of coming over to Delhi. "It is" he said, "a most thoughtless act of the hysterical in the extreme. You were perhaps disappointed when I declined to accept your services as a nurse to accompany me to Delhi and stay there for a month. But, he continued, "my whole position in public life is built upon my reputation as a man of character and unsullied morals. If my enemies are afraid of me and respect me it is because of this. I can never be a party to damage it in any way. If it was damaged the whole purpose of my life would not only vanish but my people for whom I have lived and sacrificed and who rightly or wrongly think that I am their God would be destroyed.

"The long and short of it" is he observed, that if some circumstances compel me to depart from my resolution, I may marry but will not agree to keep a nurse or companion, especially when there is no other woman in the house. It may be a long search for a woman who could be a satisfactory wife to me." (*Last Few Years of Dr. Ambedkar:* Ibid., pp. 76-77)

What happened in between Sharda and Ambedkar only they know or God knows. Ambedkar wrote to Chitre: "I have decided to marry Sharda Kabir. She is the best match I can find. Right or wrong, the decision is made."

Ambedkar also informed his trusted lieutenant Gaikwad about his marriage. Although after the death of his first wife, he had resolved not to marry again, he had now decided to marry. He wanted an educated lady who knew cooking and was a medical practitioner. As it was quite impossible to find such a lady among the members of the scheduled castes, he chose Sharda Kabir.

When Bharat Ratna Prof. P.V. Kane, who was Ambedkar's teacher, came to know about the intention of his pupil to marry Sharda Kabir, he wrote a letter to Ambedkar in which he said: "The lady you are going to marry is not at all a worthy match. You had better marry a prostitute who will regain her social status in the society. To marry this lady will not have good effect on your reputation, name and fame." (*Last Few Years of Dr. Ambedkar:* Ibid., p 190)

Dadasaheb Gaikwad also told Ambedkar that to marry this lady would have an adverse and far-reaching effect on our people.

In spite of such a stern warning from his teacher, a person of the stature of Bharat Ratna Kane and his trusted lieutenant Gaikwad, Ambedkar married Dr. Miss Sharda Kabir on 15 April 1948 at his residence in New Delhi under the Civil Marriage Act in the presence of his few personal friends.

After the marriage, Sharda Kabir changed her name to Mrs. Savita Ambedkar. It may be noted that Sharda Kabir was fond of changing her name as easily as changing clothes, such as Sharda, Laxmi, Leela etc. After the death of Ambedkar, she adopted another name, viz. Bitoo, in 1960 to conceal her identity and to carry on her affairs. (Ibid., p. 206)

The New York Times described the marriage as more significant than the wedding of a royalty to a commoner.

Terry Pilchick observed: "Ambedkar married twice, first at the age of 14 and again at the age of 56—his first wife having died in 1935. The first marriage was arranged by his father and was quite naturally within his own caste. But his second marriage was, as he put it, the best match he could arrange for himself. He married a Brahmin doctor. But the match was not popular among his followers. Again and again I saw the same photograph of his first wife—perhaps the only one ever taken—mounted on the walls of Buddhist households. She was revered as an archetype of loyalty, patience and devotion. But the popular mind turned sharply, even vindictively, against his second wife. (Ibid., pp. 199-200)

The observations of Terry Pilchick speak of the regards for Ramabai and disregard for Savita.

What havoc this Saraswat Brahmin woman played in the evening of the life of Ambedkar has been narrated in minute detail by Nanak Chand Rattu, who was very close to Ambedkar, in his book, *Last Few Years of Dr. Ambedkar.*

Justice Mulik Jiwanlal Kapoor, who was then a Judge of the Supreme Court of India, remarked: "Dr. Ambedkar had been cruelly deceived and robbed. This lady was not at all a suitable match befitting his status and grand personality." (Ibid., p. 190)

In utter disgust, one day, Ambedkar told Savita: "After I am out, either to the office or to Parliament House, you wander away the whole day in the car, meeting Brahmin officers and ministers at their residences. Are you here to see the 'Kumbha Mela' or to serve me? You had promised that you will dust out the books and place them before me on the table. You had also promised that you would look after me well and pay more attention to my meals, but I find that you get no time from your wanderings. Did I not also make it clear to you, before the marriage, that there is not the least sexual urge or feeling left in me, which has altogether died? You have not the least interest in reading and writing, nor the time to look after me. You are here only for merry-making and enjoyment. I have studied you very well for the last one year. Those very rascals have deceived me, in the lame excuse that you will look after and serve me." (Ibid., p. 191)

It is evident from what Ambedkar said that at that age and stage of his life, he had neither weakness nor attraction for sex. Then what was the mystery in marrying a Brahmin woman of the character of Savita? It seems to me that she must have been planted by the rascals mentioned by Ambedkar.

It may be recollected that Ambedkar had made up his mind to renounce Hinduism and embrace Buddhism. The Brahmin brains must have sensed that if Ambedkar lived long, he would convert not only scheduled castes, but also a majority of the Hindu population to Buddhism, which would not take much time to see the eclipse of Hinduism.

Ambedkar did embrace Buddhism on 14 October 1956 at a mammoth gathering in Nagpur and converted over five lakhs of his brethren to Buddhism. And the way in which conversion after conversion was to be followed he would have probably brought a sizeable population of India into the fold of Buddhism. The unfortunate and untimely death of Ambedkar set this fear at rest.

Nanak Chand Rattu on page 207 of his book, *Last Few Years of Dr. Ambedkar* says: "I would like to record here with a bit of hesitation that in case I make revelations of all her (Savita) affairs with the available material, information, documentary evidence, my personal knowledge and bitter experiences in plenty, the reader may stop reading, place the book aside, bow his head with moist eyes, so visibly moved, and with a long sigh exclaim, 'Ah! Babasaheb, Babasaheb, Babasaheb you were destined to such a sad tragic end. I will not, however, do that, rather my conscious does not allow me.' "

K. Krishnamurthy, who was an ardent admirer of Ambedkar, wrote a letter to him on 22 March 1956, which he concluded thus: "I am now fully convinced and I concur with Madam Bastien [who had specially come from France to give a course of treatment based on Cosmic Radiation to

Ambedkar] that if at all anybody is to be held responsible for your premature disability—and God forbid—your earlier death, it will be only due to your own indifference to face reality that it is your Mrs. who is the enemy of your welfare. You are completely ignorant of the reality of the various forces around you. If we are fortunate, which I doubt very much, you will realize the gravity of the situation early, break off the shackles that chain you to the advices of your Mrs. and undertake the course of treatment suggested by Madam Bastien."

Krishnamurthy made desperate efforts to meet Ambedkar on 25 March 1956, but he was not allowed. He sent a letter to Ambedkar on 26 March 1956 in which he wrote: "My heart bleeds when I see you struggling with your legs. I feel whether I could cut off my legs and give them to you. The allopathic doctors have been treating you for nine full years and yet you could not get even an iota of improvement. Unfortunately, to my spiritual reading, it is your own people, especially your own Mrs., who is the root cause for this unhappy state of affairs. If things continue like this unchecked, I am afraid, you will have a shorter life than what we all wish. It is up to you to think of the lakhs of scheduled castes whose uplift is dearer to you than the pleasures of family life."

Krishnamurthy concluded his letter by saying: "If you are convinced of the treatment and if you feel like continuing it, you may intimate me through your secretary as to the exact time I can come and attend on you, but there should be no interference from your wife." (Ibid., pp. 224-25)

What Nanak Chand Rattu and Krishnamurthy have said will lead any rational mind to infer that Sharda Kabir came in the life of Ambedkar under the garb of his second wife not to nurse and cure him but to bring him premature death to accomplish the ulterior motives of the rascals who made Ambedkar marry her.

4

Buddhists in Precept—Hindus in Practice

It may be recollected what Ambedkar had written to Sanghrakshita on 30 October 1956 immediately after his initiation to Buddhism. "I am glad that you realize that having begun the task well, we have to look to its continued progress in the future. We have to consider ways and means of imparting knowledge of Buddhism to the masses who have accepted His Dhamma and will accept it on my word. We should no doubt train a large number of workers to teach the Dhamma to the people, but the best agents for carrying out the same are the Bhikkhus. They would carry a great deal of prestige with them which no lay man could do.

"The Bhikkhus in my judgement ought to be very happy to find out that a large task awaiting them has been done. The only difficulty with the Bhikkhus is that they do not care to learn the language of the people. I am afraid the Sangha will have to modify its outlook and instead of becoming recluses, they should become like the Christian missionaries, social workers and social preachers. As I told you, today they are neither *Arhants* nor useful members of the society. This fact must be hammered into them and make them realize that they could serve the Buddha well by becoming preachers of His Dhamma.

"I like your idea of opening a sort of logical Seminary where Bhikkhus and non-Bkikkhus could be taught the fundamentals of Buddhism and made to learn the different languages of India so that they could be sent to the different parts."

Strangely enough Sangharakshita did nothing to follow Dr. Ambedkar's advice, and also none else, for the matter.

There are quite a big number of Bhikkhus in India today appearing not so much from the need of the community as from their own individual commitments to Buddhism. A few of them have received training and most have little idea, if any, of what the spiritual life is about. Some of the older ones were Hindu sanyasis before the conversion; afterwards they simply got themselves ordained as monks so that they could continue their undemanding lives undisturbed.

Giving the reasons for the decline of Buddhism, R. R. Diwakar, in his book *Bhagwan Buddha* said: "The virtual disappearance of Buddhism as such from India after about fifteen centuries is one of the most baffling problems in the history of this land. Why did it disappear from the land of its birth, after dominating it for some centuries and disseminating the doctrine to all the parts of the then known world? Of the various reasons suggested, many of which have some truth in them, the most important may be said to be the decline of vigour in the Sangha, its gradual transformation while adopting itself to the way of the masses, the absorption of some of its main principles such as renunciation and *Ahimsa* by Hinduism, the opposition of the vast majority of the Hindu community, and the Muslim invasion.

"The decline of vigour in the Order or the Sangha was a major cause of the decline of Buddhism. The vitality of the Sangha lay in the spirit of renunciation, self-discipline, broad mindedness, liberality, service and sacrifice for the many. When those characteristics weakened and are almost lost, the influence of the Order disappeared. Buddha himself, right up to the last days of his life, went on from one place to another inspiring and arousing the people and leading them to the noble path of righteousness. Sariputta, Moggallana and numerous other Arhant disciples of his followed the same ideals. As time went on, the Buddhist monks did their best to live up to those high principles and succeeded in converting a big part of the known world to the sublime doctrine of the Buddha. In India, great kings and emperors embraced Buddhism and with zealous devotion worked for the preservation and spread of Dhamma. By the eleventh century after the Buddha (sixth century A.D.) there were great universities and centres for study throughout the country, some with as many as 10,000 students from every Buddhist land. Kings, nobles, merchants and the common people all contributed their share towards the maintenance of these institutions; but although these rich endowments and the royal patronage made the Buddhist organizations strong and prosperous, they, at the same time, gradually deteriorated the high ideals of renunciation and sacrifice on which the Sangha and the universities were founded. The monks in course of time became used to an easy life devoted primarily to academic pursuits and religious celebrations; they grew lax and accepted perverse and worldly practices and beliefs which were contrary to the earlier ideals, and which hardly differed from those of the masses. This led to the disintegration of the Order into diverse sects, to the weakening of the moral standards of the Sangha, and to a corresponding waning of their influence on the people as well as to a gradual decline of the religious fervour, faith and devotion of the laity."

Diwakar further added: "Another important factor in the decline of Buddhism in India was the strong opposition from the orthodox Hindu traditionalists. The orthodox members of the community had always been against Buddhism, chiefly because of the loosening of their own hold on the masses. During the glorious days of Buddhism, under the protection of royal patronage, the sectarian Hindus could not raise their voice against Buddhism, but after its decline, the orthodox community was able to move without restraint and slowly converted Buddhist temples; the Buddhists, lacking a strong leadership and subject to the surrounding community pressures, were slowly absorbed. In those parts of India which were not brought under the control of the Muslim invaders, the pressure of the caste system slowly brought about the end of Buddhism."

Had Ambedkar remained alive for some years, he would have certainly emulated Buddha and moved from one place to another to inspire and arouse people for the revival of Buddhism in India. Unfortunately, he passed away in just seven weeks after his conversion to Buddhism.

Buddhist Seminary

Ambedkar had conceived an idea of setting up a Buddhist Seminary at Banglore in 1954 on a piece of land donated by the Maharaja of Mysore. But it could not see the light of day during his lifetime. The proposal, though not dead, has not been brought to shape by the so-called followers of Ambedkar.

The voice of Buddha seems to have whispered in the ears of Vimalakitti Gunasiri, telling him not to run away from the struggle, but to face it, and to see in life ever greater opportunities for growth and advancement. Otherwise how could he establish a Buddhist Seminary in Nagpur in 2006 under the name of *Mahanag Sakyamuni Vijjasan*, that too in the fierce opposition to the extent of driving him out of Nagpur by the followers of Ambedkar?

Today, the same Buddhist Seminary has been recognized by the Government of Maharashtra as a college affiliated to the Nagpur University. Vimalakitti is now set on establishing another Buddhist Seminary in Mumbai. His non-sectarian attitude of looking at Buddhism has attracted youths from all castes and communities for training as Bhikkhus.

Vimalakitti is a person, who has dedicated himself right from his prime youth for the cause of teaching true Buddhism in India and abroad. He has overcome all temptations to lead an affluent worldly life to become a monk. He has unflinching faith in Lord Buddha and Bodhisatva Dr. Babasaheb Ambedkar. But with a heavy heart, during his talk with me on 26 June 2010 in Mumbai, he said:

"Unfortunately, the followers of Ambedkar have made Buddhism synonymous with Mahars. They consider themselves to be Buddhists by birth."

Vimalakitti edits a magazine in Marathi under the title, *Vijit Sangram* in which he writes thought-provoking editorials and articles. His editorial, "Bauddha Samaj Kothe Aahe?" (Where are Buddhists?) in the issue of April-May 2010 and his article under the caption, "Ambedkari Chalwaliche Audit," (The audit of Ambedkar movement) are eye-openers and provide enough material for the introspection of those who claim to be converted Buddhists and follower of Ambedkar.

In his editorial, he writes: "In Maharashtra Buddhists are those who were earlier Mahars. They, on the top of their voices proclaim themselves to be Buddhists, because of which it is in general presumed that if he is a Buddhist, he must be a Mahar and vice-versa. This has made Buddhism synonymous with Mahars."

The followers of Ambedkar should study the editorial and the article written by Vimalakitti which are given as Annexures II and III in this book before it becomes too late.

After the Mahaparinirvana of Ambedkar, one admits it or not, the wave of Buddhism has faded and I am afraid it will continue to fade further unless serious efforts are made to halt it.

Both Buddha and Ambedkar have been effectively deified by many. They have become the objects of prayer for procuring a son, a promotion, to pass an examination and so on. Paliks have been seen with the burst of Ambedkar on festival days. In the same way many other confusions have crept into the practice of the Dhamma. Bhikkhus take the place of Purohits. Paritran chanting takes place during the Satyanarayana puja. Buddhavasi takes the place of Kailasvasi and so on.

Buddhist monks who chant the couplets wishing the marriage a success do it in a manner reminiscent of the Hindu marriage. The contents of the couplet are different but the tune is the same. The customary offering of betel leaf and betel nut to the assembled guests is still an important item in the marriage. The converted Buddhists, instead of putting red ochre on the forehead of the guests, put blue powder. Amongst the Hindus, the guests bless the couple by throwing turmeric-coloured rice. The neo-Buddhists do it with flowers. The marriage seasons and timings correspond to that of the Hindus.

Legality of Buddhist Marriages

An appeal was made by Smt. Baby against Jayant Mahadeo Jagtap in the Hon'ble High Court of Bombay under Hindu Marriage Act 25 of 1955), Section 2, 7 (2) read with Section 3 (a)—a customary form of marriage amongst members of the Buddhist community converted from scheduled castes sometime in 1956—Validity (Penal Code (1860), Section 494); custom-members of scheduled castes in Maharashtra converted to Buddhism form of marriage).

In this appeal the complainant, the first wife, challenged the order of acquittal, acquitting both the respondents for having committed offences punishable under Section 494 read with Section 109 of the Penal Code. Both the complainant and accused were members of the scheduled castes and were converted to Buddhism some time in 1956, i.e., prior to their marriage in 1971. The case of the complainant was that the accused married again in 1976, when the first marriage was subsisting. The question involved in this appeal was a question of considerable importance affecting a large number who had chosen to convert themselves into the Buddhist faith. The question was one of recognition in law of the customary form of marriage different from the generally recognized under the Hindu Law. The form of marriage was as follows:

"The bride and the bridegroom, after taking their bath and after wearing new clothes, are brought to the marriage hall. In the marriage hall the photographs of Lord Buddha and Dr. Babasaheb Ambedkar are placed on a chair and those photographs are worshipped and garlanded by them. Thereafter, both bride and bridegroom stand with folded hands before these two photographs and after respectfully bowing to these photographs recite the following:

" '*Buddham Sharanam Gacchami, Dhammam Sharanam Gacchami, Sangham Sharanam Gacchami.*" ' Thereafter separate ceremony and mantras, i.e. *Mangala-sutta,* are recited. The bride and bridegroom garland each other and take oath to the effect that as wife and husband they will henceforth conduct towards each other happily; that they shall conduct their family relations with happiness. After this oath is taken, the people who are present in the marriage hall shower flowers on the bride and bridegroom and thereafter the betel leaves and betel nuts are distributed among the guests, and the band is played."

The appeal was heard by Hon'ble Justice Bhonsale. In his judgment said: "According to section 2 of the Hindu Marriage Act, 1955, 'Hindu' includes persons converted to Buddhism and since the customary rights and ceremonies among this community have been what the witnesses have described them to be, it was not possible to put the validity of these forms of marriages in the straightjacket either of 'Saptapadi' and 'Lajja Homa' or of this custom not being ancient within the meaning of Section 7 (2) read with Section 3 (a) of the Act. If a different and new form or variation in these ceremonies and rites of marriage were adopted by a particular community, the law had to take cognizance of the same at some point of time and accord them recognition in the eye of law. The refusal to recognize the solemnization of such ceremonies of marriage as a valid and legal marriage would visit these people with untold miseries of grave social consequences. Hence rites and ceremonies averred in this case and which had been consistently followed for more than 25 years amongst this community and had been uniformly observed and had not suffered any discontinuance at any point of time could be said to be the customary rites and ceremonies for solemnization of a valid legal marriage amongst the members of the Buddhist community."

Hon'ble Justice Bhonsale in his judgment referred to certain recommendations made by the Maharashtra State Law Commission in its Ninth Report on 'Some aspects of the Hindu Marriage Act 1955.' One such aspect relates to the amendment of Section 7 of the Hindu Marriage Act 1955. The Commission had recommended certain simplification of ceremonies of marriage among the Hindus as well as Buddhist communities. As several ceremonial forms are adopted by different sections of the Hindu community in this State, it was specifically pointed out that some of the marriages solemnized in such forms were not recognized by the Courts as valid marriages in the absence of performance of essential ceremonies of 'Saptapadi' and 'Lajja Homa'. One of the suggestions made in the Report of the Law Commission was with regard to the amendments to be made in Hindu Marriage Act. The amendment was suggested in the following sections:

Section 7A

1. Notwithstanding anything contained in Section 7, a Hindu marriage may also be solemnized in the presence of relatives, friends or other persons in any of the following manner:
    a) Each party to the marriage making a solemn declaration in the language understood by the parties that each takes the other to be his wife or, as the case may be, her husband, and each party to the marriage garlanding the other.
    b) By performance of any appropriate ceremony prevalent in the community to which other parties to the marriage belongs.
2. Notwithstanding anything contained in Section 7, but subject to the other provisions of the Act, any marriage solemnized in the manner provided in sub-section (1) at any time before the commencement of the Hindu marriage (Maharashtra Amendment) Act shall be deemed to have been with effect on and from the date of the solemnization of such marriage, good and valid in law.

The Law Commission stated that the proposed new Section 7A would be a step in the right direction to legalize the simpler and economic forms of marriages prevalent in different sections coming under the Hindu Code.

Hon'ble Judge directed to forward a copy of the judgment to the Government of Maharashtra, Law and Judiciary Department saying that the Government of Maharashtra should persuade the Government of India to introduce necessary amendments to the Hindu Marriage Act, 1955 as suggested by the Maharashtra State Law Commission in its Ninth Report on 'Some Aspects of the Hindu Marriage Act 1955', since the issues are affecting millions of people involving their family, social life and legitimacy of their children are involved.

The Government of India does not seem to have taken steps so far to introduce necessary amendment to the Hindu Marriage Act 1955 as suggested. (*All India Reporter,* 1981, Bombay, pp. 283-299)

One Vishnu Kumar Kardak had sought Ambedkar's guidance on Buddhist marriage ceremony. On 26 December 1956, Ambedkar informed him: "The Buddhist marriage ceremony is simple. There is no Homa and there is no Saptapadi. The essence of the ceremony lies in placing an earthen pot newly made between the bride and bridegroom on a stool and fill it brimful with water. The bride and bridegroom should stand on two sides of the pot. They should place a cotton thread in the water pot and each hold one end of the thread in their hands. Someone should sing the Mangal Sutta. Both bride and bridegroom should wear white clothes."

The presence of the photo in Buddhist Viharas and at all Buddhist functions seems to set Indian Buddhists today apart from the main Buddhist tradition. The inclusion of Ambedkar as an object of reverence is the most visible innovation in the practice of contemporary Buddhists in India. The Buddha and Ambedkar in plaster, stone, poster-art and painting, in song and drama and story, the two seemingly of near, equal importance, rarely one without the other are continual evidence that contemporary Indian Buddhism proudly combines its own tradition with that of the main Buddhist tradition. At every occasion, both figures are garlanded, the Buddha first; the incense is lit; and Bhagwant Gautama Buddha and parampujya Babasaheb Ambedkar are addressed before the speaker acknowledges the chairman of the function and brothers and sisters.

In villages, the statues of Ambedkar are seen with a book in hand indicative of the Constitution of India. The utterance of his name is a prayer. Though devoted to him, the poor and illiterate folk seem to have little knowledge of the Buddhist teachings he championed. Another broadly accepted way of honouring Ambedkar is to add the diminutive of his first name, Bhimrao to the list of Refuges, i.e. Bhimam Sarnam Gacchami, so that the three Jewels become four:

> I go for refuge to the Buddha,
> I go for refuge to the Dhamma,
> I go for refuge to the Sangha,
> I go for refuge to Ambedkar.
> (Detlef Kantowasky, *Buddhisten in Indien Heute:* pp.13,18, 21,23, 24)

Diksha

In his Diksha address, Ambedkar had said: "Only those people should embrace Buddhism, who earnestly believe in it. If they do not believe in it or it does not appeal to them, they should not embrace it."

Buddha also said: "One must not accept my law from reverence but first try it as gold is tried by fire."

Every Buddhist is expected to have Diksha and observe the three jewels: Panchasheel, eightfold path and 22 vows laid down by Ambedkar. But in practice diksha does not seem to have been made mandatory. The less said the better about the observances of three jewels. If a true survey is undertaken, the outcome would be shocking.

Hero-worship

On his Golden Jubilee celebrations Ambedkar said: "You have been celebrating my birthday for 15 years. I have never attended them. I have always been opposed to them. You have celebrated my Golden Jubilee now; let that be enough. Let there be no more celebrations." He further added: "Over regard for leaders saps self-confidence of the masses, leaves them helpless, when left leaderless in the hour of trial or when led by unscrupulous leaders.

"One great reason for the downfall of the Hindu society and the perpetuation of its degraded position is the injunction of Krishna that whenever in difficulties they should look out for his *Avatar* (incarnation) to redeem them from the touch of dependency. That has made the Hindu society helpless in the face of calamity.

"I do not want you to follow such a ruinous teaching. I do not want you to be dependent on any single personality for your salvation. Your salvation must lie in your own hands, through your own efforts."

In his message in the special issue of *Jai Bhim* published from Madras, Ambedkar said: "It is an unfortunate fact that in India, the political leader is placed on the same footing as the prophet. Outside India, people celebrate the birthdays of their prophets. It is only in India that the birthdays of the both the prophets as well as the politicians are celebrated. It is a pity that it should be so. Personally, I do not like the celebration of my birthday. I am too much of a democrat to relish man-worship, which I regard as perversion of democracy. Admiration, love, regard and respect for a leader, if he deserves them, are permissible and should be enough for both the leader and the followers. But worship of the leader is certainly not permissible. It is demoralizing to both."

In utter disregard to the advice of Ambedkar his birthday is celebrated on a grand scale. In Pune and in Aurangabad, the central point is the statue of Ambedkar near the railway station and Bhadkal gate respectively. The procession scattered from all localities are brought to Ambedkar Square. The similar is the pattern at other places.

This is nothing short of a ritual as in respect of the birth and death anniversary of Mahatma Gandhi.

The converted Buddhists and all those who are interested in Buddhism must recollect the words of Swami Vivekananda who said: "I have neither the time nor the inclination to describe the hideousness that came in the wake of Buddhism. The most hideous ceremonies, the most horrible, the most obscene books that human hands ever wrote or the human brain ever conceived the most bestial forms that ever passed under the name of religion, have all been the creation of degraded Buddhism." (Swami Vivekananda, *My India: The India Eternal*, pp. 133-34)

The *Vedas* say: "Wake up, stop not until the goal is reached....Be courageous. Do not try to lead your brethren, but serve them. The brutal mania for leading has sunk many ships in the waters of life. Take care especially of that, i.e., be unselfish even unto death and work."

Although Ambedkar did not believe in the *Vedas*, yet this should be the spirit and determination to revive Buddhism in India. And this can be done only by following the advice of Lord Buddha when he said: "Go unto all lands and preach the gospel. Tell them that the poor and the lowly, the rich and the high, are all one, and that all castes unite in this religion as do the rivers in the sea."

Joint Movement Launch

In his Diksha address, Ambedkar had said that some people in India would say that Buddhism is the religion of the untouchables. They would malign and pass disparaging remarks. He had also said that the Mahars should do nothing that would bring them a bad name. They must lead such a life that they may command respect. They should not think that this religion is like the dog-collar tied to their neck.

It is for the neo-Buddhists and the followers of Ambedkar to ask themselves the following questions:

Whether they have not made Buddhism the religion of the untouchables? What do people in general think about them today? Are they looked upon with respect or contempt? Have they not tied Buddhism round their neck like a dog-collar?

Have they not made the conversion a laughing stock? Their conscience will tell them the truth.

However, it is not too late to act upon the advice of Ambedkar. Ambedkar's advice to his followers was: "It is your duty to raise Buddhism to a better status. You should act in a manner so as to enthuse and inspire respect among other people. You should endeavour to follow Buddhism sincerely and always keep in view the position it had once attained. If you do not do so, people will laugh at this conversion."

We should keep the ideal of Yasha before us and find how he became the disciple of Lord Buddha and what he did to preach and spread Buddhism. To refresh the memory, I give below some details about Yesha:

Yasha

In Benares there was a millionaire's son named Yasha, who led a luxurious life. One morning he rose early and, to his utter disgust, saw his female attendants and musicians asleep in repulsive attitudes. The whole spectacle was so disgusting that the palace presented the gloomy appearance of a charnel house. Realizing the vanities of the worldly life, he stole away from home, saying, "Distressed am I! Oppressed am I!" and went in the direction of Isipatana where the Buddha was temporarily residing, after having made the five Bhikkhus attain Arahantship. This took place on the fifth day after the delivery of the first sermon when all the five Bhikkhus had attained Arahantship.

At the particular time the Buddha, as usual, was pacing up and down in an open space. Seeing Yasha coming from afar, he came out of his ambulatory and sat on a prepared seat. Not far from him stood Yasha, crying. "O distressed am I! Oppressed am I!"

Thereupon the Buddha said, "Here there is no distressed, O Yasha! Here there is no oppression, O Yasha! Come hither, Yasha! Take a seat. I shall expound the Dhamma to you."

The distressed Yasha was pleased to hear the encouraging words of the Buddha. Removing the golden sandals, he approached the Buddha, respectfully saluted him and sat on one side.

The Buddha expounded the doctrine to him, and he attained the first stage of sainthood (*sotapatti*).

At first the Buddha spoke to him on generosity (*dana*), morality (*sila*), celestial (*sagga*), the evils of sensual pleasures (*kamadinava*), the blessings of renunciation (*nekkhamman-isamisa*). When he found that his mind was pliable and was ready to appreciate the deeper teachings he taught him the Four Noble Truths.

Yasha begged the Buddha to grant him the lesser and the higher ordination.

"Come O Bhikkhu! Well taught is the doctrine. Lead the holy life to make a complete end of suffering." With these words the Buddha conferred on him the higher ordination.

With the Venerable Yasha the number of Arahants increased to six.

Yasha had four distinguished friends named Vimala, Subahu, Punnaji and Gavampati. When they heard that their noble friend had shaved his hair and beard, donned the yellow robe, and entered the homeless life, they approached and expressed their desire to follow his example. Yasha introduced them to the Buddha, and, on hearing the Dhamma, they also attained Arahantship.

Fifty more worthy friends of Yasha, who belonged to leading families of various districts, also received instructions from the Buddha, attained Arahantship and entered the Sangha.

Hardly two months had elapsed since his enlightenment when the number of Arahants rose to sixty.

With these sixty pure ones as the nucleus, the Buddha founded a celibate order. They were drawn from the highest status of society and were all educated and rich men, but the Sangha was open to all worthy ones, irrespective of caste, class or rank. Both young and old, belonging to all the castes, were freely admitted into the Sangha and lived like brothers of the same family without any distinction. The noble order of the Bhikkhus, which stands to this day, is the oldest historic body of celibate in the world.

The outlook of people at the age-old Buddhism expounded by Lord Buddha and the one revived by Dr. Babasaheb Ambedkar is at variance although the goal of the two is the same.

There is a dire need to bring fusion between the age-old Buddhism and neo-Buddhism. Both are making efforts to achieve the goal in their own way. But if they join hands and launch a joint movement to give jet speed to the revival of

Buddhism in India keeping in view the approach of Buddha, the results will be spectacular.

Set up a Buddhist University

We need to organize a huge machinery for the propagation and intensive spread of Buddhism. We will have to impart teaching in Buddhism and train a large number of Bhikkhus to reach the message to the people in various parts of India as advised by Lord Buddha. For this purpose we should set up a Buddhist university at Aurangabad which was one of the three ambitions of Ambedkar. The proposal may sound to be a dream but if we mobilize forces and resources it may come true.

5

Rise and Fall of Ambedkar's Political Parties

Independent Labour Party

Ambedkar formed Independent Labour Party in 1936 on the pattern of the British Labour Party. In his interview to the *Times of India* on 11 November 1936, Ambedkar said: "The party would endeavour to educate the masses in the methods of democracy, place before them the correct ideology and organize them for political action through the legislation."

Commenting upon the programme of the Independent Labour Party, an English daily wrote: "The new party which Ambedkar just organized in the province could be of considerable use in developing the life and moulding the future of the country. Emphasizing that there was both scope and need for such a party, and hoping that it would, together with the socialists, present a strong defence against the sweeping tide of communism, the new party will be one of the most powerful political groups in the country." (Dhananjay Keer, *Dr. Ambedkar- Life and Mission,* Popular Prakashan, pp.286)

Bombay Legislative Assembly

Ambedkar contested the election of 1937 to the Bombay Legislative Assembly, where there were 175 seats out of which

15 were reserved seats, which Ambedkar found insufficient to create a powerful opposition. He therefore decided to field some more candidates of his choice for the general seats. He also supported a few independent candidates.

Ambedkar himself contested from Bombay. The Congress fielded Palvankar, the famous Indian bowler of those days. The Congress also pushed in the arena, P.N. Rajbhoj and Deorukhkar to sabotage Ambedkar's chances. The election took place on 17 February 1937 and Ambedkar won the a election with a landslide victory to the utter disappointment of the Congress.

Overall out of 17 candidates put up by the Independent Labour Party, 15 were elected, a grand success to the credit of the newly formed political party.

Work in Bombay Legislative Assembly

Ambedkar was sworn in on 9 July 1937 as a member of the Bombay Legislative Assembly. The Congress members took the oath of allegiance to the British King. Ambedkar refused to swear by the *Bhagavad Gita*. He solemnly took the oath.

Ambedkar continued to be a member of the Bombay Legislative Assembly till the Assembly was prorogued in 1939 when the Second World War broke out.

During the short tenure of two years, he expressed his views on the following Bills, which speak for his study, vision and relevance for India of the twenty-first century:

1937

Ministers' Salary Bill (23 August 1937); The Hereditary Offices Act Amendment Bill (17 September 1937); The Bombay

Hereditary Offices Act (21 October 1937); Bill to Abolish Khoti System (21 October 1937).

1938

Local Boards Act Amendment Bill 1 (18 January 1938); Probationer of Offenders Bill (20 January 1938); Local Boards Act Amendment Bill 2 (22 January 1938); The Small Holding Bill 2 (24 January 1938); Budget 3 (2 March 1938); Tobacco Duty Act Amendment Bill (5 March 1938); Independence of Judiciary Bill (7 March 1938); Creation of Separate Province Bill (4 April 1938); The Bombay Primary Education Act Amendment Bill 1 (21 April 1938); The Bombay Police Act Amendment Bill 1 (27 April 1938); The Bombay Police Act Amendment Bill 2 (28 April 1938); The Bombay Police Act Amendment Bill 3 (29 April 1938); The Bombay Primary Education Act Amendment Bill 2 & 3 (30 April 1938); The Bombay Municipal Act Amendment Bill (3 May 1938); The Assembly Procedure Bill (10 September 1938); Industrial Disputes Bill (15 September 1938).

1939

Budget 4 (21 February 1939); Disturbunces Enquiry Committee Report (17 March 1939); The Finance Act Amendment Bill (28 August 1939); Participation in the War 1 (25 October 1939); Participation in the War 2 (26 October 1939); Participation in the War 3 (27 October 1939).

The detailed views expressed by Ambedkar are in Volume 2 of his *Writings and Speeches* published by the Government of Maharashtra.

Ambedkar's views on Ministers' salaries, the creation of separate Karnataka Province and industrial disputes and strikes are prophetic and therefore they are given below in brief.

Ministers' Salaries

Speaking on the Ministers' Salaries Bill moved in the Bombay Legislative Assembly on 23 August 1937 Ambedkar said: "What are the considerations that ought to prevail in the fixing of the salary of a minister? In my judgement, Sir, there are four considerations which ought to prevail. The first is consideration of the social standard of the ministers, who are undoubtedly the social leaders of the community; secondly, considerations of competency; thirdly considerations of democracy; and, fourthly, considerations of integrity and purity of administration.

"The ministers of the country, who are the first citizens of the country, should lead a life which is cultured, which cares for art, which cares for learning, and which ought to be a model for the rest. But if our friends do not care to consider that aspect of case, as I say, I am prepared to leave it out of consideration altogether. But surely the consideration of competency, the consideration of democracy and the consideration of integrity could never be overlooked in fixing the salaries of the ministers.

"If the view is that the ministers are to do nothing more than go about and unfurl flags and receive salutes from crimson clad ladies forming guards of honour, then that is a different proposition. In my view, and I want to emphasize it with all the emphasis I am capable of, if there is anything we expect from the ministry, it is competency. I have no doubt in my mind that of the three organs of the state—the legislature, the executive and the judiciary— the executive is the main spring of action. It is the executive which is to study the problems that are facing the country; it is the executive which is to show what solutions can be proposed for solving those problems. In short, Sir, it is the executive that must be the brain trust, if we are to solve the various problems with which we are faced and to get the best out of this Constitution.

"The question that arises in my mind is this, whether the salary that is proposed is a salary which is capable of inviting men who are capable and who have the necessary competence to face problems and suggest remedies. Looking at the question dispassionately in the light of the circumstances which I see prevalent in this country, I cannot give, Sir, an affirmative answer. First of all, there is this fact to be considered, namely, that there are other walks of life in which the prizes are far greater than the prizes that have been provided for the ministry. Many people who have competence, who have ambitions, will seek other walks of life rather than come to the ministry and have the responsibility of Ministry. I would have understood if the ministry was legislating that nobody should receive a salary more than rupees five hundred in any walk of life. If they had done so, things would have been otherwise, but they are not doing so. They are driving away competent men to other walks of life. This is one aspect of the matter. The second aspect to be considered is this. Looking at the situation in India, I cannot help saying that the intellectual class from which you can draw men who are competent enough to undertake the responsibility is very small.

Sir, in this country, on account of the social system which has been prevalent and which the British regime has not been able to damage very much, education was confined to a small class. Education has never been the privilege and opportunity of many. In fact, under the Chatur Varna, it is only one who could take education and the rest were debarred. Consequently, a large mass of the people are absolutely so situated that they cannot throw forth leaders who can be taken in the ministry to carry on the administration. Therefore, my submission is that the salary is not a salary which can invite competent people to carry on the administration.

"Coming to the question of democracy, what will be the effect of the salary? I would not mince matters. I would straightway say that the consequence of this salary will be this: Either there would be people who do not care for money, who have private means but who want to capture political power in order that they may use that political power for the advancement of their own class or their own community. That would be one consequence. The other consequence would be that men who cannot make any money in other walks of life will get into the ministry. There can be no other consequence.

"I have no hesitation in saying that that will be the consequence of this Bill. There can be no greater disaster if what I apprehend comes true. We want that the political power which is given under the Government of India Act should not be cornered or monopolised by a few who have money and who do not care for salary. Nor do we want in the interest of the masses that the power should go into the hands of incompetent people.

"Coming to the other question, namely, the integrity and purity of administration, a friend of mine who is Congress-minded said one thing which I would like to repeat on the floor of this House. He said that if the Governor were to give him a contract for the supply of ministers, he would very readily undertake the contract and also give something to the Presidency of Bombay for giving him that contract. I think, Sir, that remark is very pregnant. There are hotels in Europe who pay to the managers to allow them to wait. That shows what responsibilities there are open to people who are not kept above the temptation to pick something which they cannot get by way of pay.

"Even with higher salaries I admit, and readily admit, that you can never buy the dishonesty of the dishonest man. That is, however, not the consideration. The consideration is whether you cannot fix the salary in such a way that the minister will be kept beyond temptation. Sir, we have had in this province a salary of Rs. 4,000 and a salary of Rs. 3,000, and yet there were scandals that have been produced in the past. In this, the question that arises for consideration is not merely whether the salary is adequate. But my view is that it is not the close of the argument. The problem of salary has to be considered from two points of view. From the standpoint of the individual the consideration is one of adequacy. From the standpoint of the state the consideration is a consideration of safety and purity of administration. A man may say that a particular salary is adequate salary for him. But it does not follow that you should not consider whether from the public point of view is a safe salary. The lowest standard is not necessarily a safe standard. I believe my friends opposite will have, when they give contracts, to enter a clause that contracts shall not be given merely because the tenders are the lowest; Just as we do not give contracts to persons simply because their standards are the lowest, similarly we cannot allow persons to serve as ministers merely because they are prepared to accept the lowest salary. We have to consider the other side of the question, whether the contractor who is offering the lowest tender is capable of discharging the obligations of his task. Therefore, I am suggesting that, though the Honorable minister may say that Rs. 500 salary is good enough, it does not dispose of the argument. The House has to consider whether on this basis it can expect and hope to have an administration which is free from the corruption that may be possibly arise.

"What are the principles that have been suggested for the salary that has been fixed in the Bill? The one thing I have heard often said is that the salaries ought to be in accord with the income of people. I ask the question, if that is so, can it be said that Rs.500 salary is in accord with the income of the people? What is the income of the people? I have here figures given in the *Harijan*—I suppose a standard authority—from which I may quote.

"According to the figures given here, the income per head in the United Kingdom is £ 50 per annum; in the United States of America, £ 100; in France, £ 40; in Australia, £ 70; in Canada, £ 75; in India, £ 4. Now, Sir, if all this is done on the principle that salaries ought to be in accord with the income of the people, then I do not understand how it can be suggested that the salary of Rs.500 a month is in accord with the £ 4 income of the people in this country. Surely if my honourable friend is basing the Bill which he has placed before us, on this principle, namely, that the salary should be in accord with the income of the people, then Rs.500, I submit, is a most extravagant sum to take for the Ministry; it ought to be less than Rs.100; it ought to be Rs.75, as we suggested. If they are honest, if they want to fix this sum as a matter of justice and not to placate the people, then why not be logical in your honesty? Why fix a sum which is out of all proportion to the income of the people? The second thing that has been suggested in justification of the low salary is that the ministers ought to live in such a manner that they should look as though they were of the people, that there should be no distinction between ministers on the one hand and private citizens on the other.

"Sir, if this is the object of the ministry, that all distinctions should be abolished, that they should look as though they were of the people, that the people should have full confidence in them as though they belong to the people, then, my submission is that this is not the method of winning the confidence of the people. Sir, in this country, the cleavages, social and religious, are far greater than they exist anywhere else in the world. We have here—I am speaking of this presidency for the moment—we have the division of Brahmins and non-Brahmins; the division of the touchables and the untouchables, I am confining myself again to Hindus, we have the division of Maharashtrians versus Gujaratis; we have the division of Gujaratis versus Kanarese. And add to all that the difference between the Hindus and the Muhammedans. If you want to create confidence in the administration, then I submit that the proper way of doing it is not for the ministers to go about in the streets half clad, showing their anatomy; or smoking bidis in place of cigarettes; or going in third class or in bullock carts. Nobody is going to be deceived by these things. If you want to gain confidence of the people, then, I submit that the only way of doing it is to constitute your government, your ministry, your civil services, in such a way that it does not become the monopoly of any particular class or any particular community. We shall watch what the ministry is going to do about it. But if they want to pretend that they are going to create confidence by doing these, what I might call, puerile things, then, I submit it is an attempt that is doomed to failure.

"Then, Sir, the ministry has come forward with what might be called an act of renunciation on their part. It reminds me of the conduct and the way of life of medieval monks. The medieval monks, when they started their careers as monks, were required to take the three vows—the vow of celibacy, the vow of chastity, and the vow of poverty.

"I do not know whether my honourable friends have taken the vow of celibacy. I suppose it is too late for them now to do it. I do not know whether they have taken the vow of chastity. But if they have and if they break it, it is certainly not the matter of grievance for this House. But certainly they have taken the vow of poverty, as I see from this Bill. Can they keep this vow? The medieval monks very seldom succeeded in maintaining their vow of chastity, but they always succeeded in maintaining their vow of poverty.

"I venture to say that this Bill is not put forth out of any pious motive; there is a strategy behind it. That strategy is this, that they should always remain in the saddle and nobody else should take their places.

"Dr. Johnson said that patriotism was the last refuge of the scoundrels. He could very well have said that politics in India should become the last refuge of the scoundrel that I have risen to speak."

If we cast a dispassionate eye on the members of parliament and legislatures, we will find the truth in what Ambedkar had said about them. Our elected members seem to be more interested in their own welfare rather than the welfare of the masses. The ascending graph of their pelf and power will bear testimony to it.

Creation of a Separate Karnataka Province

"We, representing the scheduled castes, take no pride either in being Maharashtrians or Gujaratis or Karnatakis. For reasons which I need not enter into on this particular occasion, there are very many reasons why we do not think that it is not our land. However, I am using the argument in order to show to the House that by circumstances, I am capable of taking a dispassionate view of the situation that has been presented to us by this resolution. Sir, it would be necessary and desirable for members of this House to bear in mind one fact which I think is of supreme importance. This presidency of Bombay was, before the Act came into operation, composed of four different units: Gujarat, Maharashtra, Karnataka and Sind. This joint family has not been together for the last 115 years. Sind was with us for nearly 90 years. It has been separated. It is a matter of fact that we have been living together for the last 115 years only to emphasise on the fact that those who want this unity to be sundered, that these three parts which are together be now separated, must consider this matter in a much more serious way and not on grounds which are purely sentimental.

"The first thing I propose to consider is this. Our friend who has moved this resolution has given expression to the view that the proposition is only a part of a larger whole, the ideal being the unification of all Karnataka people, that this resolution is merely a step in that direction. Now, Sir, the question that I would like to ask on this aspect is this. It is likely that this ideal, if my honourable friends will allow me to say, this dream could be realized, the ideal of all Kannada-speaking people coming together? I have no doubt that this is a dream which can never come true, and the reason for my saying so is this.

"I have no pride in being a Maharashtrian, but the fact remains, and when I use it, I do want to caution the House that I am not citing it by the way of complaint, that it is not my object; I am not citing it merely to point out a fact. The fact remains that the minority people, namely, the Gujarati-speaking and the Kannada-speaking people have not been done any injustice either in the matter of seats or in the matter of offices. Before this matter was discussed in this House, I told my honourable friend, Mr. Jog, quite plainly, that if he proved to my knowledge and to my conviction that the Karnataka people suffered in any way, either they did not receive adequate and just representation in this House or that they did not receive sufficient representation in the Cabinet.

"Speaking for myself at any rate, I do not see that the Karnataka people have suffered in any way by their remaining within the presidency of Bombay. The separation of the province might satisfy the ambitions of few people who want to figure as the heads of the province but what about the rest of the population who need to be fed, who need to be clothed, who need to be housed? None of us can tolerate this kind of thing. I do say that with all emphasis, Sir, after all, what are these districts? Two of these districts are famine-stricken. The whole of Bijapur is a famine-stricken district. The whole of Bellary also, I am told, is famine-stricken. What revenue does he expect to get from the famine-stricken area? Merely by separating from the Bombay Presidency, is that going to milch a cow?

"Then there is another question to which I advert and it is this: I being a member of a minority, I am bound to consider these things from the standpoint of the minority. I am very glad that several members who spoke in favour of the resolution did give us an assurance that the interests of the Muhammadans and the interests of the Harijans will be looked after. But I do want to say this, that along with dismemberment of these provincial areas there is going to be a dismemberment of the minorities. I cannot forget the fact that in Karnataka we have only two seats. I am sure that those members of scheduled castes who came from Karnataka must be feeling that their strength lies in the fact that there are 13 members from other parts of Presidency to look after them. What is to happen to them? I am sure, for instance, the Muhammedan community has got about eight seats from Karnataka.

"I won't argue as I am rather pressed for time. But we cannot allow this kind of dismemberment. It is very good for the members of the majority community to say that they will be generous and they will be kind. We cannot depend upon their generosity and upon their kindness. We want rights and rights cannot be given in a generous way. To a community which after all on a purely population basis forms only a microscopic minority, even supposing they were prepared to give weightage, what weightage could they give to a population which is about a few lakhs? This is one of the points on which I support this resolution. This dismemberment I am not prepared to accept. Our strength lies in a polyglot administration. I do not want to say. But I have my fears that if Karnataka is created as a separate Province, it would be province of all the Lingayats against everybody else. I am not mincing matters, but if, for instance, there was separation there would be a combination of the Marathas against the Kanarese, we don't want this kind of thing- and there cannot be a common front which we at present enjoy.

"I know there are people probably who would not agree with me but that is my conviction that the British, whatever they may have done in the course of history, whatever they may have failed to do—and there are many things which they have failed to do, which their self interest probably did not permit them to do-have done two things which I am generous enough to admit has been two monuments of their rule in this country which will survive even when they go away. The one thing that they have done for us is a common code of law. You can travel from Kashmir down to South India and know that murder is the same thing whether you commit it in Kashmir, Punjab and the North-West Frontier Province, or whether you commit it in Rajahmundry in Madras. You know what Transfer of Property means; you know what evidence means wherever you go. Sir, I say such a thing we did not have. The other thing that the British have done is that they have given us a common central government. Such a thing we did not have before. The importance of this fact of having a common central government is not probably realized by all. But I think it is a very crucial fact. If today we are on the way of building a common nation, a spirit of nationality, a feeling that we are all one, it is due to the fact that we have a common government; it is due to the fact that we realize that we are citizens of common government.

"Sir, I would plead with the members of this House that they should do nothing whereby they would impair these two advantages which we have secured. Personally myself I say openly that I do not believe that there is any place in this country for any particular culture, whether it is Hindu culture, or a Muhammedan culture, or a Kanarese culture, or a Gujarati culture. There are things we cannot deny but they are not to be cultivated as advantages, they are to be treated as disadvantages as something which divides our loyalty and takes away from us our common goal. That common goal is the building up of a feeling that we are all Indians. I do not like what some people say, that we are Indians first and Hindus afterwards or Muslims afterwards. I am not satisfied with that, I frankly say that I am not satisfied with that. I do not want that our loyalty as Indians should be in the slightest way affected by any competitive loyalty whether that loyalty arises out of our religion, out of a culture or out of a language. I want all people to be Indians first, Indians last and nothing else but Indians and, therefore, I say that this is a resolution which directly runs counter to this ideal. Sir, this is an ideal which we ought to cherish zealously. I can quite understand that in a country like America, in a country like Germany, in a country like Europe, where the feeling of oneness is solidified, where there is no need to make anybody feel that he is not a German to tolerate anything that is of a separatist character, but where the feeling that we are Indians is still in its embryo is only beginning to ripen, to allow other loyalties, feeling of culture, feeling of nationality to grow simultaneously, I say deliberately-is the greatest crime that we can commit and I, for myself, will not be a party to it and I strongly, very strongly, oppose this resolution."

The creation of provinces after provinces, instead of proving a blessing, have been proving a curse. They have albeit been satisfying, as stated by Ambedkar, the ambitions of a few who want to figure as the heads of the provinces. But at the cost of making the vast majority of the population poor and poorer and rich richer. And there is the least hope that the wisdom will prevail on power mongering politicians to stop playing with the sentiments of people to create new provinces under the garb of Linguistic States. One should not be surprised to see in the distant future, the present day satraps ruling the states as erst-while Maharajas ruled their states (kingdom). I am afraid that the ultimate result may be revival of the East India Company in the form of multinational corporations.

Industrial Disputes and Strikes

"It has been said that there is no such thing as the right to strike. My reply is that this statement can come from a man who really does not understand what strike is. If members are prepared to accept my meaning of the word 'strike' as being nothing more than a breach of contract, then I submit that a strike is simply another name for the right of freedom; it is nothing else that the right to the freedom of one's services on any terms that one wants to obtain. And once you concede to the right of freedom, you necessarily concede the right to strike, because as I have said, the right to strike is simply another name for the right of freedom. A sort of ridicule is sought to be poured upon it by saying that this is something like the divine right of kings. Sir, I would only say in reply that a poetic phrase or a picturesque description does not dispose of an argument; I have never seen that result anywhere, certainly not in courts of law. If you accept that the right of freedom is a divine right, then I contend that the right to strike is a divine right. I go further and say that because ten people or twenty people or two hundred people simultaneously declare a strike that cannot make any difference in the situation so far as the law is concerned.

"The Bill really, in my judgement ought to be called 'The Workers' Civil Liberties Suspension Act'. That would be the proper title for it. Some have got the impression that, after all, the suspension is only for two months—until the conciliation proceedings are terminated—and after that the workers would be at liberty to strike if they wish. Sir, I would like to say that this would be a very wrong impression. My contention is that the provision of this Bill, when they are set in operation, will bring about perpetual slavery and the workers will never be able to strike. Let us look at the provisions. First of all, the Bill provides that when Act comes into operation, there is not to be any strike at all for one year. Whether conditions are such that a reasonable worker would accept them or whether conditions are such that no reasonable worker would accept them, for one year there is complete slavery. The workers are bound down to the terms mentioned in the second Schedule. There is no escape; there is no going away from that position. What happens after the first year is over? What happens is this. You have got to give notice; that takes away a part of the time during which you cannot strike. Then after notice is given, time is allowed for reply. During the period of reply you cannot strike. Then, conciliation proceedings commence. They may last for two months, if the parties are fortunate, if the parties are reasonable; but the Bill provides that the term may extend to four months. Therefore, from the date of the origin of the grievance of the workers, for four months and practically 25 days—I will stand corrected if my calculation is wrong because I have not gone into the details—the worker must do nothing. He must not talk, he must not deliver a speech, he must not organize, and he must do nothing. All mobilization included a word or a speech or an action is penalized during this period. "Suppose that no conciliation is effected during this long period of four months and 25 days—I submit a long period of gestation—what is to happen? The worker is allowed only two months to strike after the conciliation period is over. I do not know whether my honourable friend the mover of the Bill thinks that two months is a sufficiently long period for the demobilized forces of labourers to mobilize for action. I have been an active worker in the labour field. I cannot say that I am a field man and I therefore do not know what are the difficulties which a person who is organizing the workers for strike will have to meet. But looking at the situation from such experience as I pass as an observer in the City of Bombay, I have not the slightest hesitation that two months would be the most inadequate period for a body of labourers who have been held at bay so to say, for four months and 25 days to mobilize their forces in order to strike. If they do not strike within two months, what happens? What happens is this that they are deemed in law to have accepted the situation. If they again raise their head and find out new grievances, the law says you shall again wait for four months and 25 days and allow conciliation to go on. Wait and see what we do. Wait and see, for four months and 25 days. Again if nothing happens at the end of four months and 25 days, if you think you can strike, do so within two months. If you do not and after two months you raise another grievance, you shall have to wait again for four months and 25 days. Sir, I would like to know whether such an endless cycle of don'ts would not produce complete slavery, perpetual slavery, of the workers for all time. If this is not a Bill for introducing slavery amongst workers, I would like to know what sort of Bill would introduce slavery?

"It will be necessary and I say very instructive to compare the provisions of this Bill, in so far as they relate to strike, with the provisions contained in Trade Disputes Act of 1929. That is an Act which also imposes certain limitations upon the right to strike and it would be, therefore, very instructive to compare the provisions contained in that Act with the provisions contained in this Bill, so that the House may be in a position to realize in what direction we are moving, whether we are moving in the direction of slavery. Sir, the Act of 1929 imposes certain limitations upon the right of workers to strike and it would be enough if I refer to two of its sections. That Act of 1929 penalizes a general strike for political purposes. That is Section 16 of the Act and the other section which is more relevant for my purpose is Section 15 which penalizes a strike without notice. Apparently there does appear to be some sort of similarity between the Act of 1929 and the present Bill in so far as this Bill also penalizes a strike without notice. But, Sir, beyond that the one Bill is as different from the other as chalk is from cheese. The one has nothing to do with the other and, comparatively speaking, I have not the slightest hesitation in saying that this Bill is reactionary and retrograde, and that the author of this Bill is a far greater Tory than the author of the Act of 1929.

"This has always been the view taken, that if you want to restrict the right to strike and to make it illegal, then you must do it only in relation to services on which the sustenance of the life of community depends. Now, it is obvious that this Bill extends to every trade and every industry. I do not wish to say anything with the object of making fun, but I should like to illustrate my point by saying that, supposing tomorrow the Indian women—I hope they do not—adopt the fashion of painting their lips and some manufacturers who had a nose for money started an industry for making lipsticks for supplying their needs, and if under this Act the workers went on strike, its provisions would fall upon their head like the sword of Damocles. Can anybody seriously maintain that the lipstick industry is essential to life, that the right to strike should be curtailed because some women are deprived of the pleasure of having the usual paint of their lips? Sir, this government has not only let go by the broad attitude it took in 1929, of restricting the penalty to strikes in social security services, but they have beaten the bureaucracy by going beyond the provisions of the Act of 1929. The bureaucracy had at least the sense, if I may say so, the responsibility, to realize that the right to strike was so important that it should not be penalized beyond the four corners of what was covered by public security; and here is a Bill which, I would like to repeat, would make a strike in the lip-stick industry penal.

"All this, for what? What are we to gain by all these trials and tribulations which they are trying to impose upon these poor workmen? The result, as I see, is to wait at the table of some gentlemen, whom the Bill calls the conciliator, for 4 months and 25 days. Beyond that I see nothing.

"With all the provisions that they have got, they should have bucked up, they should have had the courage and said, 'We shall compulsorily arbitrate, whether you agree to it or not.' It is another matter whether I agree or not. If you had taken up that attitude, I could have certainly understood it, because the position that would have been this, that at the end of 4 months and 25 days you would have been certain of some tangible result.

"What is all this for? You have to go through several stages—a Registrar, a Conciliator, and a Board of Conciliators if both parties agree. It is only a case of securing appearances before certain amiable gentlemen who will talk sweetly to different people and bring about probably a good temper, if a hungry man who wants something can be said to be in a good temper. I do not see anything in it. This is, in my judgement, absolutely in futility, an utter futility which can have no tangible result at all. The only tangible result of this will be that this delaying process for 4 months and 25 days will disable the worker from going on strike ultimately.

"If this democracy—well, it might be, but I do not say it is democracy—a democracy which enslaves the working class, a class which is devoid of education, which is devoid of the means of life, which is devoid of any power of organization, which is devoid of intelligence, I submit, is no democracy but a mockery of democracy. So much for the main provisions of the Bill.

"Then, Sir, there are certain other provisions if the Bill to which I wish to advert, and these provisions are contained in clauses 4 to 20. Looking at the clauses, they refer to four different topics. They refer to different clauses of unions, qualified unions, registered unions, representative unions. Sir, I had the opportunity of reading the previous draft of this Bill. That previous draft had a different phraseology, such as horizontal unions, vertical unions, diagonal unions and perpendicular unions. I am glad that that phraseology has been dropped.

"The second thing with which these clauses deal is the terms and conditions the procedure with regard to the registration of the different classes of unions. Thirdly, the terms and conditions and the procedure for these recognized unions or registered unions to be declared representative unions, and fourthly, the conditions for the registration of a union and for the cancellation of its declaration as a representative union. Now, Sir, I have been considerably at a loss to understand what practical connection these clauses have with the main provisions of the Bill. The main provisions of the Bill are, firstly, compulsory conciliation and, secondly, penalty for strike during conciliation proceedings. To my mind, I do not see any organic connection between these clauses and the other clauses in dealing with these two topics which are the main purposes of the Bill. And, referring to the title of the Bill, I found that rather than disclosing the purpose it tries to conceal it. The Bill has a title which says 'A Bill to make provision for the promotion of peaceful and amicable settlement of industrial disputes by conciliation and arbitration and for certain other purposes'. Sir, what are the other purposes? And why have they not been specified in the title of the Bill? Is it something of which one need feel ashamed? I do not know. Either there is some practical connection between the two parts of the Bill or there is not; if there is that ought to have been disclosed, and if there is no organic connection, then the logical conclusion is that these sections ought to be deleted from the Bill. But, Sir, my search has been rewarded by the discovery that there is an organic connection between the two. What that organic connection is, will be readily by reference to clause 75 of the Bill. Clause 75 of the Bill says: 'No employee shall be entitled to appear in any proceedings under this Act except through the representative of employees.'

"Sir, this clause is the most fundamental and I say this is the most destructive clause of all trade unionism in India. Who is a representative of employees who is entitled to represent labor in conciliation proceedings? No one will have any locus standi in any negotiations for the settlement of an industrial dispute, no matter what his qualifications may be, unless he falls within the definition of what is called by this Bill as a representative of employees, and it is for the purpose of defining who is a representative of labor my honorable friend has introduced Clauses 4 to 20 in the Bill. They all hang on this section. The important question, therefore, is who is a representative of employees under the Bill?

"Now, Sir, under this Bill, there are two categories of unions which will have the right to represent labor. The first is a union which has 20 per cent of workers as its members, or rather not less than 20 per cent of the workers as its members, and recognized by the employer. Secondly, a union whose membership is more than 50 per cent can represent labour in the conciliation proceedings. These are, therefore, the two categories of unions which alone have the right to represent labour. Now, Sir, my honorable friend the Minister chooses to call them 'representative unions'—both of them. I disagree with his terminology. I think a spade ought to be called a spade. Calling a spade a spade, what I submit is this: there is, no doubt, two kinds of representative unions under this Bill, but the important point to note is that one is a slave union and other a free union. Sir, there is no exaggeration and there is no violence done to language if I say that a union which can have *locus standi*, a legal existence, a right to represent and a right to speak, only if it secures the prior approval of the employer is a slave union and a union of freemen. I wish he had used the word 'approval'; the word 'recognized' is very inappropriate; the proper definition should have been 'a union approved by the employer', as we would then have seen in plain term what we are asked to give our sanction to.

"What is happening today in this country of our? I am sorry I have to make a plain breast of what I feel on this occasion. We have mills in Bombay City managed by Parsis. There are mills managed by Gujratis. There are mills in Bombay which are managed by Jews or by Europeans.

"The most surprising thing about all these mills is that they have been made the heaven for the cousins of the managers. Hundreds of useless people are employed in higher grades simply because they are related to the managing agents in some way. You go to a Parsi mill, you will see hundreds of Parsis employed whether you wanted it or not. Go to a mill managed by Gujaratis. You will see hundreds of Gujaratis employed whether you wanted it or not. Go to a mill managed by Jews. You will see hundreds of Jews employed, whether you wanted it or not. The best part of earning of the worker is taken away by the managers in order to feed these people who are employed in the mills, whether they are efficient or not, or whether they wanted or not. All these people who are controlling the industry float the capital and bloat it up by all sorts of paper transactions. When the worker says that he gets less wages, the man controlling the industry says, 'It is my capital'. All this is bogus capital, stock exchange capital, bolstered up by spectaculars. A good part of the earning of the industry is swallowed by these people. From the title balance is left, the workers are asked to eke out their existence. If the Honourable the Prime Minister wants to introduce equity, let him make the workers' wages the first charge in the profits of industry. I do not understand why the mill owners or, for the matter of fact, any owner of any industry, should not be required by law to present his budget annually.

Government is required to present its budget every year· annually we get a budget of government in which the government say how many Ministers are employed, how many chaprasis are allowed to the ministers, how many superintendents, are there in departments, how many clerks, this, that and the other. This House is in a position to understand whether the establishment is excessive or not. This House gets to know whether the money is spent properly or not. Why it is that a mill owner or, for the matter of fact, the owner of the industry, who gets his earning, not entirely by his capital but also by the sweat of another man, be not compelled to give the details of his management? This is a very fair demand to make. The advantage would be this. Once a budget of that kind is presented by the owner of an industry, the workers would be in a position to realize and scrutinize whether the balance that is left to be divisible among the laborers is fair or whether the employer has taken an undue portion of the total profit. What is the use of having a conciliation board and asking the employers to produce their account books when the employee is not placed in a position to scrutinize what is really the state of affairs? If the procedure I suggest is adopted, I am sure about is that there will be less labour troubles, the conciliation would be more effective and there will be more industrial peace."

Ambedkar's views reflect his concern for the protection of workers and labourers from their exploitation by the employers. There is hardly any difference in what Ambedkar said about the mill owners and industrialists then and now. Take any industrial empire of today built by the Birlas, Dalmias, Modis, Dhoots, Ambanis, Singhanias, Mallyas,

Kirloskars or for that matter any big or small industrial magnet. Who are reaping the harvest in the form of plums and perks? No one else but their kith and kin.

Short Life of Independent Labour Party

The Independent Labour Party was, however, short-lived despite the fact that it fared well in the 1937 elections by winning 15 of the 17 seats that it contested. The reasons for the short life of Independent Labour Party were various. One of the main reasons was that the support base of the party was restricted largely to Mahars, which is evident from the fact that the majority of the candidates fielded were Mahars. Contrary to this the Congress Party chose its candidates from non-Mahar untouchables like Mangs, the Dhors, and Chambhars.

Ambedkar realized that his move towards uniting the working class for creating a strong joint front was unrealistic since it was very difficult to transcend caste divisions in the working class. Therefore, he came to the conclusion that class factors could only emerge to become the basic unit of struggle once caste has been destroyed. These factors led Ambedkar to abandon the Independent Labour Party model as a strategy for the organization of the depressed classes. The alternative was to rely on the untouchables alone to create an organized political force for fogging a reliable base for supporting the movement he was leading. This strategy reflected the belief that the untouchables could not rely on non-untouchables for the support and solidarity in their political movement, but had to develop independent organization, which would be concerned exclusively with issues peculiar to them. The result was the formation of the All India Scheduled Castes Federation in July 1942.

Dhananjay Keer in his book, *Dr. Babasaheb Ambedkar: Life and Mission,* at page 343 writes: "The new policy of Britain in regard to the Depressed Classes compelled Ambedkar to make a departure from his new role as a labour leader. During the interview Cripps asked Ambedkar whether he represented the labour or Depressed Classes and also asked him about the strength of his party. That gave turn to his role; and once again Ambedkar thought it wise to resume the leadership of the Depressed Classes in the interest of his people for whom he had been fighting all along the past twenty-five years. He, therefore, convened on March 30 and 31, 1942, a conference of the leaders of the Depressed Classes who were present in Delhi and held consultations with them on the Cripps proposals. M.C.Rajah, who had up to that time opposed Ambedkar, was now reconciled with Ambedkar. Rajbhoj had already joined him. It was decided, after a gap of ten years, to hold an All-India Depressed Classes Conference at Nagpur, in July 1942, with a view to creating an All-India organization with distinct aims and purposes in cooperation with all the inter-provincial forces."

All India Scheduled Castes Federation

The All India Depressed Classes Conference was held at Nagpur from 17 July to 20 July 1942. Reportedly, it was attended by not less than 75,000 men and 20,000 women as representatives of the depressed classes from all the provinces of India.

Expressing his happiness over the deliberations of the conference, Ambedkar emphasized the need for forming an All India Political Organization to act as the only mouth piece of the untouchables of India with provincial branches abolishing all the existing organizations. "This will," he said, "give you the strength you need to enable you to work in a manner that will help you to build a united front." He further said, "My great desire is that there should be buildings of our organization not only in each province but in each town to serve as a center of office and activities."

Ambedkar continued: "My final words of advice to you are educate, agitate and organize. Have faith in yourself. With justice on your side, I do not see how you can lose the battle. The battle to me is a matter of joy. The battle is in the fullest sense spiritual. There is nothing material or social in it. For ours is a battle not for wealth or power. It is a battle for freedom. It is a battle for the reclamation of human personality."

Protesting against the charge to the effect that he was indifferent to the society and lived among books, Ambedkar said: "That he had no ill feeling against anybody and he never meant any insult to anybody. He had to achieve maximum progress in minimum time. Many Hindus regarded me as their enemy. But I have personal friends from even the Brahmin community. Situated as I am, it has fallen to my lot to lash the anti-social actions of the Brahmins, who treat my people worse than dogs and cats and impede their progress." (*Dhanajay Keer, Dr. Ambedkar, Life and Mission,* Popular Prakashan, Mumbai, pp. 351-53)

Ambedkar followed George Bernard Shaw who said: "Life is no brief candle for me. It is a short of splendid torch which I have got hold of for the moment, and I want to make burn as brightly as possible before handling it on future generations."

The All India Depressed Classes Conference then resolved to form the All India Scheduled Castes Federation as the central political organization of the Depressed Classes and appealed to all local political organizations of the depressed classes to merge into this central organization to work through it. Rao Bahaddur N. Shivaraj was chosen as its first president.

Nanak Chand Rattu in his book *Last Few Years of Dr. Ambedkar* on pages 44 and 45 writes: "Ever since its inception, the Federation commanded the support of the scheduled castes. It being their only organization, it induced confidence, enthusiasm and hope. The response to clarion call of their leader was so great and spontaneous that it exceeded all expectations so much so that the scheduled castes all over India rallied around the Federation and made it their only representative organization. It progressed mainly due to the devoted, dedicated workers who ceaselessly struggled hard to the building up this organization. The Federation vehemently worked for their political demands, got them the place of honour and dignity and filled in them consciousness and awakening and the urge to govern and not to be governed by those who had exploited and enslaved them for centuries untold."

While Ambedkar was still in Nagpur, he received a message that he has been included in the Viceroy's Executive Council as a member in charge of Labour and CPWD.

Member of Viceroy's Executive Council

Ambedkar was given reception in the evening of 17 January 1943 by the Marathas and allied communities at Bombay. In the course of his address, he traced the causes that led to the downfall of the non-Brahamin political parties, which were in power in Bombay and Madras for 20 years. He said that the first cause was that the non-Brahmin parties prostituted their position for providing jobs. They had no broad-based policy, no broad-based measures that benefitted the masses of their followers, the peasants and labourers who were their main supporters. What was equally tragic was that those men who were given jobs by the non-Brahmin parties, when put in the saddle, forgot the class from which they came and became as insolent and arrogant as foreigner. Democracy failed in its full purpose in the West because it was in Tory hands. The same would be the position in this country, if Brahmin minority came to power. He then told that three things were essential for making a political party powerful. The first was that its leader must be so great as to be a match for the leaders of other parties; the second essential was a disciplined organization; and the third was a clear-cut programme. These requisites should be fulfilled if democracy was to succeed in India and to be rescued from the hands of the Torries."

Addressing the Chamber of Commerce on 10 May 1943, Ambedkar said: "The world was sick of war and suffered from three diseases, namely, Imperialism of one nation over another; colour bar; and poverty.

As to the problem of poverty, he expressed at the horror of thought of the sky-soaring daily expenditure the nations incurred in destroying the civilization of man. He said he could not understand why Britain, who spent Rs 14 corers per day and the USA, who expended about the same amount as also

India in her way enormously, should not spend half of it on liquidation of poverty in peace time to better the lot of the suffering humanity. The world will have to make amends, will have to surrender and give up some of the cherished privileges in order to abolish poverty.

Enumerating the benefits he had secured since his taking office as Labour member, Ambedkar told in November 1943, in New Delhi, the leaders and the workers of the depressed classes that he had secured eight and half percent appointments in government posts, reserved seats for technical education of the depressed class students in London and one more seat in the central assembly and got one created in the Council of States.

Ambedkar's insistence on securing a fixed percentage of government posts sprang from two considerations. He was absolutely convinced that but for the caste Hindu predominance in government services it would have been well-neigh impossible for the caste Hindus to perpetuate tyranny over the depressed classes. Secondly, the government jobs increased the possibility of their getting justice in government dealings in addition to raising their economic status.

Kanpur Session of Scheduled Castes Federation

In his address to the annual session of the Scheduled Castes Federation at Kanpur on 29 January 1944 Ambedkar declared: "the Government of India must be shared by the Hindus, Muslims and untouchables; and if the untouchables did not get a proper share in the conduct of the national government, they would launch a struggle to achieve that object."

Releasing the *People's Herald* a weekly organ of the scheduled castes, at Calcutta in January 1945, Ambedkar stressed the importance of the Scheduled Castes Federation and added it would be an eternal party in the country from the political and moral point of view and because elevation of the scheduled castes was the noblest work a leader could find in India, he had devoted himself to it.

General Elections of 1945

The Viceroy, Lord Linlithgow, announced general elections in September 1945. All the political parties entered the election fray. On 4 October, Ambedkar made a beginning of the election campaign at a meeting in Pune. He emphasized that the depressed classes should not play in the hands of the Congress leadership, which was full of surrenders; it was tool in the hands of capitalist, and those socially indifferent; it never strove to remove their disabilities, and to redress their grievances. The remedy lay in their hands and therefore they should capture the political power which was their life-blood. They should develop into a ruling race and guard their rights. Otherwise, they would remain on paper. In the end, he said that the coming elections were a matter of life and death for them; and more so, because the Constitution-making body was likely to be elected by the provincial legislatures.

The election propaganda was launched by the Scheduled Castes Federation with greater vigour. To give an impetus to the election campaign, a provincial conference was held at Ahemdabad on 29 and 30 November 1945. Ambedkar told the conference that whatever benefits they were enjoying had been secured by him, and not by Gandhi, who had sought the help of the Muslims to oppose their demands.

Ambedkar made a tour of South India to give filling to the election campaign. He addressed meetings at Madras, Madurai and Coimbtore.

Ambedkar came to Bombay on 13 January 1946 and left for Sholapur. Addressing a public meeting at Sholapur, he declared at the top of his voice that if the Scheduled Castes Federation candidates were not elected, he would surrender to the Congress, wear a white cap and work under the Congress. Such was the confidence of Ambedkar in the victory of Scheduled Castes Federation in the election. However, the results of the elections were shocking. The Scheduled Castes Federation was completely routed and Ambedkar was left to bite his own teeth.

General Elections of 1952

Ambedkar tried to infuse new life in the All India Scheduled Castes Federation before the First General Election held in 1952. The executive body of the Federation met at his residence in Delhi in the first week of October 1951 to draft the Parties Election Manifesto. The Manifesto was finalized as given below.

1. The Scheduled Castes Federation will not ally itself with a Political Party which has not laid down its principles and whose principles are not in antagonism with those of the Federation,
2. The Federation will not support the independent candidates,
3. The Federation would like to work in cooperation with the Backward Classes and the Scheduled Tribes, they

being more or less in the same position as the Scheduled Castes,

4. The Federation will not have any alliance with any reactionary party such as the Hindu Mahasabha or the R.S.S.,
5. The Federation will not have any alliance with a Party, like the Communist Party the objects of which are to destroy individual freedom and Parliamentary democracy and substitute in its place a dictatorship,
6. The Federation having no belief in totalitarian will not join a political party which is already totalitarian and which will not permit Opposition Party to grow,
7. Federation is opposed to the growth of multiplicity of Political Parties- the party to be somewhat on the lines of the British Labour Party which is a Federal Party,
8. The Federation is prepared to be a unit of such a Federal Party provided it has its Principles set out in clear terms; the principles of such a party should not be opposed to the principles of the Federation; the Party seeking the alliance must pledge its support for the social and economic uplift of the Scheduled Castes; the Party must agree to permit Scheduled Castes Federation to function as an autonomous unit within the Federal Organization in the matter of its internal affairs and the Party must not be affiliated to any party which is not recognized by the Federal Party as a unit of its own and
9. The individuals who seek the aid of the Federation would be required to become Associate Members of the

> Federation and sign a pledge to the effect that they accept the principles, the policy, the programme and the discipline of the Federation.

On the evening of October 27, 1951, after inaugurating the election campaign at Jalandhar, Dr. Ambedkar addressed a special session of the "Political Scientists Parliament" at D.A.V. College. Speaking on the occasion he sounded a note of warning that if parliamentary democracy failed in this country—and it was bound to fail because of the attitude of the party in power— rebellion, anarchy and communism would be the only result. Then the fate of this country would be doomed.

Speaking at length he cited many rules about parliamentary procedure—elaborating, "that at one time India had parliamentary institutions and that there are innumerable references in our literature to prove that parliamentary system of government was not unknown to us—that parliamentary government means negation of hereditary rule. No person can claim to be hereditary ruler. Whosoever wants to rule must be elected by the people from time to time. He must obtain approval of the people. Hereditary rule has no sanction in the parliamentary system of government.

"Secondly, any law, any measure applicable to the public life of the people must be based on the advice of the people chosen by the people. No single individual can presume the authority that he knows everything, that he can make the laws and carry the government. The laws are to be made by the representatives of the people in the parliament. They are the people who can advise the man in whose name the law is proclaimed.

"Thirdly, the parliamentary system of government means that at a stated period those who want to advise the head of the state must have the confidence of the people in themselves renewed....This is also not enough. The parliamentary system of government is much more than government by discussion. There are two pillars on which the parliamentary system of government rests. Those are the forums on which this mechanism works. Those two pillars are (i) an opposition and (ii) free and fair elections.

"For the last 20 to 30 years we are acclimatized to one single political party. We have nearly forgotten the necessity and importance of Opposition for the fair working of parliamentary democracy. We are continuously told that Opposition is an evil. Here again we are forgetting what the past history has to teach us. You know that there were 'Nibandhkaras' to interpret the *Vedas* and *Smritis*. They used to begin their comments on *shlokas* and *shutras* by stating firstly the 'Purva-Paksha', the one side of the question, they used to follow it up by giving the 'Uttar-Paksha', the other side. By this they wanted to show us that question raised was not an easy question; it is a question where there is dispute, discussion and doubt. Then they used to give what they termed as 'Adhikaran' where they used to criticize both the 'Pakshas'. Finally they gave the 'Siddhant'—their own decision. Here we can find that all our ancient teachers believed in two-party system of government.

"One important thing in the parliamentary democracy is that people should know the other side if there are two sides to a question. Hence a functional opposition is required.

Opposition is the key to free political life. No democracy can do without it. Britain and Canada, the two exponents of parliamentary system of government recognize this important fact and in both countries the leader of Opposition is paid salary by the government. They regard the opposition as an essential thing. People of these countries believe that the Opposition should be as much alive as the government. The government may suppress the facts, the government may have only one-sided propaganda. The people have made provision against this eventuality in these two countries.

"Free and fair election is the other pillar on which parliamentary democracy rests. Free and fair elections are necessary for the transfer of power from one section of the community to the other in a peaceful manner and without any bloodshed. In olden times, if a king died, there was at least one murder in the palace. Revolutions used to take place in palace resulting in murders before the new king used to take the reigns of his country into his authority. This has been the history of India. Elections must be completely free and fair. People must be left to themselves to choose those whom they want to send to the legislatures."

"Now the question arises as to whether there is any desire on the part of the party in power to permit any Opposition to be created. Congress does not want any Opposition. Congress is attempting to gather people of sundry views under one canopy. I ask you whether this is a desirable trend in the political life of this country."

He also charged the government servants of helping the party in power and said: "We also find that the government servants are influencing the elections in favour of the party which is feeding them and their dependents. No less a personality than Dr. Shyama Prasad Mookherjee at the inaugural session of the Bharatiya Jan Sangh at Delhi recently, openly charged the government servants of helping the Congress and thereby nullifying the elections from being free and fair. Under these circumstances, do you, gentlemen, think that there is any hope for the parliamentary democracy to succeed...."

Denouncing the role of 'Big Business' trying to play a great part in the political life of this country, Ambedkar said, "It is a very dangerous thing. If moneyed people try to influence the elections by contributing to the election fund at any political party, what will be the result? If the party to which they have supported financially comes into power they will naturally try to extract concessions for themselves either by modifying the present legislation or by influencing the party in power to legislate in such a manner as would be beneficial to their interests."

Ambedkar came to Bombay on 18 November 1951. He was given a grand reception jointly by the Scheduled Castes Federation and the Socialist Party. Negotiations had been going on for the electoral alliance between the leaders of the Peasants and Workers Party and leaders of the Scheduled Castes Federation on the one hand and the Socialist Party and the Scheduled Castes Federation on the other hand. Jayaprakash Narayan and Ashok Mehta of the socialist party met Ambedkar and discussed the new opposition strategy.

Ambedkar characterized the Peasants and Workers Party,

Hindu Mahasabha and Jana Sangh as communal parties and therefore refused to have alliance with them.

The Scheduled Castes Federation joined hands with the socialist party and made an election alliance in November 1951. Ambedkar addressed a joint meeting convened by Scheduled Castes Federation and Socialist Party on 25 November 1951 at Shivaji Park in Bombay, which was attended by about two lakh people. Ambedkar impressed upon the audience the need for a strong opposition to keep effective check on the party in power. "Numbers do not matter. It is the quality of opposition that counts," he said. He made an appeal to the people to elect at least the best, if not all of the candidates jointly put up by Scheduled Castes Federation and Socialist Party.

Ashok Mehta, the General Secretary of the Socialist Party, told the audience that the alliance has created a new force. Jawaharlal Nehru in his speeches at Bombay and Madras denounced the election alliance of Scheduled Castes Federation and Socialist Party as unholy.

The elections to the Parliament were held in January 1952. Ambedkar contested the reserve seat from Bombay North Constituency. He was defeated by the Congress candidate. However, P.N. Rajbhoj and B.C. Kamble of Scheduled Castes Federation were elected to the parliament and the Bombay legislative assembly respectively.

The Scheduled Castes Federation and Socialist Party were swept away at the polls. Reacting to his defeat, Ambedkar said: "How the overwhelming support of the public of Bombay could have been dallied so grossly is really a matter of enquiry by the Election Commissioner." Jayaprakash Narayan was also at a loss to understand the debacle because from all account there was an overwhelming support for the Socialists in Bombay.

A few days later Ambedkar and Ashok Mehta filed election petition pleading that the propaganda aimed at influencing the electorate to cast both votes in a double member constituency in favour of the same candidate amounted to a corrupt election practice and hence these elections should be held invalid. The respondents against the petition were S.A. Dange, Dr. Deshmukh, Dr. V.B. Gandhi, Kajrolkar and others.

The hearing of the election petition commenced in Bombay before the Election Tribunal in the first week of October 1952. Ambedkar appeared in person and said that the propaganda for the wastage of votes was illegal and that it was a gross perversion of law to arouse communal feeling among the electorates. The appeal however was dismissed. (Dhananjay Keer, *Dr. Ambedkar- Life and Mission,* Popular Prakashan, Mumbai, pp. 444)

The following comment of a press on the defeat of Ambedkar is very pungent: "Ambedkar's election defeat is a heavy blow to his political ambitions and to the prestige of Scheduled Castes Federation. Ambedkar has been a failure as a politician; his great abilities have been blunted by his fanatical communalism. He cast himself for the role of Messiah of the untouchables. His election speeches were full of rancor and half truths. He descended to demagogy and has forfeited much of the respect due to his talents. It is absurd for him to say that his people are not given a fair deal in free India. Caste prejudice exists and it will take years to remove it. But it cannot be done in the way Dr. Ambedkar wants.

"He makes matters worse by constantly harping on the unhappy fate of the Harijans. There is as much poverty and misery among other sections of the population. The removal of Harijans disability will come only through the social regeneration of the whole country. But this is a point which Ambedkar ignores."

It may be noted that this defeat of Ambedkar was after he had rendered yeomen service in drafting the Constitution of India. It reveals the orthodox Hindu mind. I venture to say that had there been any Brahmin Hindu, who had done the job Ambedkar did in drafting the constitution, he would have been elected unopposed with kudos to him. But here one agrees or not the Hindu mind against a Mahar was revealed.

Ambedkar, however, was brought in the Rajya Sabha in the middle of March 1953 from the Bombay state. His entry to the Rajya Sabha was of course a back-door entry. He wanted to be a direct representative of the people in the Lok Sabha. So he contested a bye-election to the Lok Sabha held in May 1954 frm Bhandara. He was again defeated. This time it was a reaction to the stand he had taken on the Hindu Code Bill.

The defeat of the Scheduled Castes Federation along with his own defeat did not dishearten Ambedkar. He said: "The Scheduled Castes Federation lost the last general election. Consequent upon its defeat some have deserted it, some have lost faith in it. I do not share this defeatist mentality. To win seats in the election is not the ideal of the Federation. To win seats for the Federation is only a means to an end. The end is to serve those people for whom it is established. So long as the problem remains the Federation will continue in one form or the other."

He further said:

"1. The defeat of the Federation is to be welcomed. For, it has helped to drive away the most undesirable element that had entered the federation. Those who remain in Federation have a greater responsibility falling upon them. To them my message is that after the defeat the Federation may appear like a weather- torn-tree, but it is certainly not dead at the roots.

"2. The Federation has been defeated many a times in election. People seem to think that the Federation is not a body worth consideration. We suffer defeats because we are true to our principles and we are not out for sale, nor to shift from one party to another. We stick to our own. We have stood to our own and we will stand to our own.

"3. The Scheduled Castes Federation is liked by nobody. It is necessary to understand why it is so. The Federation is disliked because it is a body of warriors out to fight. And what is it the Federation fighting for? In words of the Buddha, they are fighting for lofty virtues, for high endeavour, for sublime wisdom; for those things we do wage war; therefore we are called warriors. Let not the dislike for the Federation discourage or unnerve the Federation. It should go on fighting without compromising with evil." (Nanak Chand Rattu, *Last Few Years of Dr. Ambedkar,* pp. 26, 27)

6

Revolt against Ambedkar

Ambedkar was disgusted with the functioning of the Scheduled Castes Federation. He wrote a letter to his chief lieutant Dadasaheb Gaikwad who was President of the Bombay branch of the Scheduled Castes Federation in which he said: "The disease of disunity has gone very deep and if you take action the whole thing will break up, a result, which I am sure you do not want. The best thing would be to call a meeting of the workers in the Bombay state and have the dirty linen washed before them. Rajbhoj is, of course, another head-ache. He shall have to be dealt with. 'Janta' is another problem. It has become a group paper. It must also be dealt with."

Ambedkar further wrote: "I do not propose to be at the head of the Federation. I feel, I am too old and too sick to play an effective part in politics. You people can now run the Party. You must by now learn to take responsibility, which after my death undoubtedly be yours. Why not take it right now? I cannot remain a titular head. For, in that condition I get all the blame for all the bad deeds by others which I am unable to check by my inability to move about." (Nanak Chand Rattu, *Last Few Years of Dr. Ambedkar,* p. 37)

On 18 October 1954, P.N. Rajbhoj in his capacity as the General Secretary of the Scheduled Castes Federation brought to the notice of Ambedkar that the Federation was going through the deep crisis and that as an organization it is almost at the breaking point as so many disrupting forces were working inside the Federation. He referred to the role of R.R. Bhole and his friends in Maharashtra, and said that they are carrying on open propaganda against the office bearers of the Federation and its policies. The worst of it was that Bhole was trying to bring in a cleavage between the Mahar and non-Mahar sections of the Federation. He treated the instructions given to him with contempt. Rajbhoj requested Ambedkar to take serious note of the indiscipline going on in the Party and to put a stop to it.

"Unfortunately," Rajbhoj further wrote, "I cannot have access to you as I used to have in the former days. Many of Gaikwad's letters did not reach you and that his letters too suffered the same fate. I make myself bold to say that since your marriage you seem to have been estranged from many sincere workers of the Federation, which I consider my duty to express unreservedly, even at the cost of inviting your wrath or perhaps wounding your feelings. I write this with a bleeding heart..."

N. Shivaraj, the President of the All India Scheduled Castes Federation, right from its inception wrote a letter to Rajbhoj on 18 March 1955 in which he said: "I find that the attitude of Dr. Ambedkar has far changed towards me, that in spite of my loyalty to him, and the Federation all this time, he has completely thrown me overboard, and that is the penalty one has got to pay for being too loyal to a person. This, however, does not matter for it affects me and me only. But what is more important and damaging is, as I have pointed out in the 'Statement' the manner in which my position and prestige as the President of the Federation has been outraged and my authority as the President floated. This is a matter of interest to the public and a matter in which I should vindicate myself before our community."

Shivaraj regretted: "That things should have been done over his head and behind his back, presumably on the personal authority and knowledge of Dr. Ambedkar, which he said is all improper and unconstitutional. He further said that he cannot be ticked off his position as President by Dr. Ambedkar or anybody. In any event, after what happened I must act and quickly in self-defence."

He concluded: "It was essential that the public, our community in particular, must be told as to exactly where we stand in regard to the Federation and the future. They are at present confused and lukewarm for lack of consistent and straight forward policy on the part of the Federation."

Shivaraj asked Rajbhoj to circulate his statement amongst the members of the Working Committee of the All India Scheduled Castes Federation or to convene a meeting of the committee to consider the question raised by him and to come to final conclusion.

On 25 March 1955, Rajbhoj issued a circular to the members of the Working Committee, Presidents and Secretaries of the State Scheduled Castes Federation along with the letter and statement of N. Shivaraj making it clear that there was something basically wrong in the working of the Federation. He said that he tried to persuade Dr. Ambedkar to take them into confidence before taking any important decision and also explaining him in several letters how the Federation was disintegrating due to the lack of coordination in the organization. There was no democratic functioning left in the Federation.

Rajbhoj requested that he be relieved of the responsibility of the General Secretary of the Scheduled Castes Federation with a further request to the members to express their frank opinions on the issues raised by the President to enable them to judge and to arrive at a decision whether democracy had any place in the Federation. (Nanak Chand Rattu, *Last Few Years of Dr. Ambedkar*, p. 41)

The Statement of N. Shivaraj is given below, which speaks volumes for the functioning of the Scheduled Castes Federation:

Statement, March 18, 1955

Rapid changes that are taking place around us in the political field, and certain developments that have been going on for some time past within our body politic, have cast upon me, the duty as the President of the All India Scheduled Castes Federation, to place the matter before the members of the Working Committee for their serious consideration and immediate action. I should have drawn the attention of the Working Committee to these earlier. But I did not do so, in the interests of the solidarity and prestige of the Federation, and because I did not want our dirty linen to be washed in the public.

The Federation

1. The germs of the Federation are to be found in the Madras Provincial Depressed Classes Federation established as early as the year 1947, and of which the late Dewan Bahadur Srinivasan was the president and I was the General Secretary. It was in his capacity as President that Dewan Bahadur Srinivasan was sent along with Dr. Ambedkar to the Round Table Conference to represent the Scheduled Castes. We should here acknowledge the significant work and the invaluable services rendered by Dr. Ambedkar at the conference and afterwards, which put the Scheduled Castes upon the political map of India, and for which they will ever remember him with gratitude and affection. Attempts have been made from time to time since 1927 to bring into existence an All India Organization for the Scheduled Castes, by several representatives of the Scheduled Castes. Ultimately the All India Scheduled Castes Federation emerged as the result of the huge conference in Nagpur in July 1942, and was established with me as the president. Since then I was holding the office and would have willingly given it up in favour of Dr. Ambedkar, had he not been in the Government of India, first as an Executive Counselor and later as a Minister, practically continuously for a period of nine years. This is by the way.

Ever since its inception, the Federation always commanded the support of Scheduled Castes, and even today it is the only organization amongst the people that induces confidence, enthusiasm and hope. But certain incidence, rather inexplicable, such as the following have undermined the prestige of the Federation, and have shaken the faith of our people in the strength and value of the Federation.

a) Sometimes ago, news was published in a local vernacular journal called *Oorimal* published by Sri. Ratnam that Dr. Ambedkar was elected as the President of the All India Scheduled Castes Federation. It did not matter much, because the journal has no circulation worth the name, nor did it affect me personally except that it cast some doubts, and chilled the enthusiasm of our Federationists for some time in Madras. But what is important is: "How can a thing like that happen so casually?" The change of the President of an important All India Organization; and without my knowledge or consent? In any event without going through proper proceedings, such an irregularity was allowed, and there was no contradiction of the news either from Dr. Ambedkar, who is our constitutional Pandit, or from the Working Committee.

b) A copy of Draft Constitution of the All India Scheduled Castes Federation reveals on the front page in gold print that Dr. Ambedkar is the President. Who printed it, I do not know, or was it done with his knowledge? If so, the thing has been done clandestinely and behind my back. I do not mind it personally. But our people ask me to know as to how this could happen without anyone knowing it through open formal proceedings, more so when nobody sent me a copy of the Draft Constitution.

c) The circulation by Sri. A. Ratnam of printed copies of a letter written by Dr. Ambedkar, asking for his suggestions and those of his friends on the draft Constitution. Even this was done without my knowledge and as if the President of the Federation does not exist.

d) The publication in *Thondu,* a Tamil journal run by Mr. Veeraswami, M.P. Trichinolpoly, that Dr. Ambedkar and Mr. E.V. Ramaswami are touring South India. This also without my knowledge, nor my even getting a hint of it.

These circumstances—there are a few others too—have undermined the prestige of the Federation, as a body without head or tail, a mere plaything for Dr. Ambedkar and his favourites, such as happen to be at the present moment. All these things clearly indicate that the Federation has not got any definite and positive policy except Ambedkarism. This seems to have set in, and once it has set in, it spells the doom of the Federation. I would much rather wish that the Federation is wound up rather than allow it to deteriorate into an instrument of Dr. Ambedkar fancies. It is for the Working Committee to consider this question in all its aspects, irrespective of its fear or favour of any body, and come to a decision. My future conduct and policy will depend upon your decision. One thing however is certain, and I have made up my mind that irrespective of what happens elsewhere, Madras and South India will continue to function as a separate entity, and run under the name of South India Scheduled Castes Federation.

The Depressed Classes League

2. Large sums of money are, it seems, being spent to organize the league, in Madras under the control and guidance of Sri B. Parameshwaran, Minister of Transport, Madras, and it has a body of paid workers. There is a premium on the Federationists. If he joins, he gets a higher pay, so I am told. The real point is that our members are being thinned. At a time

like this, the incidents that I have mentioned above have further cast doubt and gloom over our sincere followers. I feel morally bound to give them a definite lead and tell them what to do in the circumstances. I must tell them soon as what is to happen to the Federation. I cannot drop them like hot potato and go away. I am not selfish. The Depressed Classes League is day-by-day growing strong, and naturally, because of our weakness. In fact they all are Congressmen. There is no need to have an organization separately. It is done only to spite and keep it as a counterblast to the Federation and drive in our people, who even now as a whole do not join the Congress, bar those career politicians.

The Congress and the Communists

3. The spectacular success of the Congress in the recent Andhra elections, which have attracted the notice of the outside world, has a psychological reaction on the minds of the people, including our own. They find that the only party they can look, is the Congress. The waverers are always a legion, but the steadfast are only a handful. It always happens that way, more so in Indian Political Conditions.

The Backward Classes

4. The Backward Classes are up and doing. They have started in right earnest and carrying on their work. They form a large number and effective from the voting point of view.

In view of the above, I think it is time and it is right that the Federation must come to a decision finally and soon as to:

1. Whether to run the Federation by making any changes for the better in the organization.

2. If so, whether in the political field to align with some other party or communities such as the Scheduled Tribes and Backward Classes, and form a large organization or
3. To dissolve the Federation as it now exists, and let our members do what is good for the community in such manner as they think fit.
4. Or to wait for and merge in the Federation- to- in 1957 under the Draft Constitution of Dr. Ambedkar which however is not before us and on which we are not expected to express any opinion or give any suggestion.

Please let me have a reply soon. I have immediately to advise the followers of our Federation in Madras State and cannot leave them in the lurch. We are here; such is the feeling of our men, to run the Federation with Dr. Ambedkar if agreeable, without him if necessary. (Nanak Chand Rattu, *Last Few Years of Dr. Ambedkar*, pp. 218 to 221)

Ambedkar wrote to Dadasaheb Gaikwad on 25 March 1955 that the Federation is full of groups each fighting against another and that he was wholly responsible for the internal dissensions within the Federation, especially in Bombay. Ambedkar said that by his conduct he had shown that he cannot tolerate a rival and that for that purpose:

(1) He fought with R.R. Bhole, because he was sent to England and America whereas he was not. (2) He quarrelled with R.D. Bhandare because he had been appointed President of the Bombay City Federation. (3) He was not only quarrelling with R.D. Bhandare, but he also got hold of B.C. Kamble and

Rajbhoj to form a group to oppose R.R. Bhole, Bhandare and support their opponents although they had been wrongdoers.

Ambedkar thus held Gaikwad responsible for dissensions and intrigues in the Federation. "There is," he said, "a limit to which a man can carry his personal prick and pride. In every Party there are people who make mistakes. It is the duty of the elders to save the face of the Party and not to exploit the mistakes for personal aggrandizement and that as an elderly person it was his duty to bring all people together and make peace. Ambedkar accused Gaikwad to have started group rivalries and group fighting. He told him that he was sick of the Federation and would like to do work which is more congenial to his mind. (Nanak Chand Rattu, *'Last Few Years of Dr. Ambedkar'*, pp. 41-42)

Surprisingly Ambedkar did not make any mention of the issues raised by N. Shivaraj in his statement.

7

Republican Party of India

The death-knell of the Scheduled Castes Federation compelled Ambedkar to think that a broad-based political party was the need of the hour. He therefore decided to form the Republican Party of India to give it a national look, open to all who accepted the three guiding principles, viz., liberty, equality and fraternity.

He prepared a draft proposal for the formation of the Republican Party of India under the title, "An open letter to the people of India to support the Republican Party of India-a proposal for consideration." He circulated the letter with the Aims and Objects of the Republican Party of India as given below:

Aims and Objects of the Party

To realize the aims and objects of the Republican Party, as set out in the Preamble—justice, liberty, equality and fraternity, the attitude of the party in public affairs will be governed by the following principles:

1. It will treat all Indians not only as being equal before the law but as being entitled to equality and will accordingly foster equality where it does not exist and uphold it where it is denied,

2. It will regard every Indian as an end in himself with a right to his own development in his own way and the State as only a means to that end,
3. It will sustain the right of every Indian freedom-religious, economic and political- subject to such limitations as may arise out of the need for the protection of the interests of other Indians or the State,
4. It will uphold the right to every Indian to equality of opportunity subject to the provision that those who have had none in the past shall have the priority over those who had,
5. It will keep the state ever aware of its obligations to make every Indian free from want and free from fear,
6. It will insist on the maintenance of liberty, equality and fraternity and will strive for redemption from oppression and exploitation of man by man, of class by class and nation by nation; and
7. It will stand for the Parliamentary System of Government as being the best form of Government both in the interest of public and in the interest of the individual. (Nanak Chand Rattu, *Last Few Years of Dr. Ambedkar*, p. 48)

Ambedkar himself got in touch with Jayaprakash Narayan, Rammanohar Lohia, Ashok Mehta of Socialist Party, who were staunch political opponents of the Congress; P.K. Atre and S.M. Joshi of Samyukta Maharashtra Samiti and a few Muslim leaders.

M.R. Chaudhry, a Muslim leader from Calcutta, strongly supported the formation of the Republican Party of India. He went to the extent of saying to Ambedkar: "I do believe that in no time, this formidable combination shall be crowned with success under your leadership."

Ambedkar informed Chaudhry on 17 July 1956 that a party which can oppose the Congress was absolutely essential and that such a party must be a strong party and not a Federation of groups, which is worse than useless. "I shall," he said, "not think of joining such a Federation. It will break as soon as the election is over. If we can have a party like the Congress, with loyalty to the party and not to the group, I think the attempt is worthwhile."

Ambedkar also informed Chaudhry that it was necessary to have a personal discussion with the leaders of the scheduled castes, scheduled tribes, backward classes and the Muslims.

On 1 October 1956, Rammanohar Lohia informed Ambedkar that he was looking forward to meeting him as early as possible. "I only," he said, "wish to emphasize the utter intellectual collapse that has overtaken our country. It is necessary for a man like you to speak unreservedly." On the same day Lohia asked Vimal Malhotra and Dharmaveer to pursue the talks with Ambedkar. "My meeting" he said "with Ambedkar will be as such a tribute to the fact that the backward and scheduled castes can produce an intellectual like him as for its political consequences."

In an interview with the press on 13 October 1956 on the eve of his conversion to the Buddhism, Ambedkar revealed that his plans for the formation of the Republican Party of

India had sufficiently progressed and that the Party would come in existence before the general elections of 1957 on three guiding principles, viz. liberty, equality and fraternity. He also made it clear that the Party would be broad-based and open to all who subscribed to its principles.

He further stated that once he became a Buddhist, he would have nothing to do with the Scheduled Castes Federation. The Federation would have to decide its relation with the new Party.

While Ambedkar was gaining wide support for the formal inauguration of the Republican Party of India, he left for divine abode on 6 December 1956.

Expressing deep sorrow and grief at the untimely death of Ambedkar, Rammanohar Lohia said: "Alas! The untimely death of Dr. Ambedkar could not see the birth of the Republican Party of India as visualized by him. The loss has been inflicted at a juncture when his services were needed most by the depressed classes and the country at large at a time when the history was being re-written. He had the necessary dynamism to keep up with it and shape it with the vision that was his own."

The Republican Party of India did come into existence. But it could not become a broad-based party as Ambedkar had conceived. Nanak Chand Rattu, who was too close to Ambedkar for 17 years, in his book, *Last Few Years of Dr. Ambedkar* on page 55 says: "The Republican Party of India leadership dominated by Mahars did not bother to enlarge their base by organizing the other scheduled castes, like Chambhars, Balmikis, Maangs etc. towards whom they had developed hatred and kept their loyalty to their caste fellows- Mahars only."

Ambedkar had announced: "Before I die, I must establish a definite political direction for my people. They have remained poor, oppressed and deprived, and because of that now a new consciousness and a new anger is growing among them. That is natural. But it is also natural that this type of community becomes attracted to the communism. I do not want my people to fall under the sway of the communists."

It was to escape the danger of being sucked into communist embrace that led the formation of the Republican Party of India. However it was driven with differences leading to splits from its very inception.

8

Educate, Agitate and Organize

'Educate, agitate and organize' was the mantra given by Ambedkar to his brethren to arouse their conscious to free themselves from the age-old tyranny of the Hindus.

Ambedkar firmly believed that education could bring not only new consciousness among the downtrodden people, but also impel them towards a praxis of self-liberation. His commitment to education was so deep and wide that it had affected the entire gamut of his activity and perspective.

He made a beginning of his movement of ameliorating the conditions of the downtrodden of India by establishing the Bahishkrit Hitkarini Sabha on 20 July 1924. After four years in 1928, he established the Depressed Classes Education Society. He opened hostels for untouchable students under these two institutions at Sholapur, Panvel, Thane with a view to creating awareness amongst the untouchable people and educating them for improvement in their socioeconomic standard.

This served as an inspiration for starting hostels in Pune, Nasik and Dharwar. Although these hostels helped spreading the primary and secondary education among the untouchables, they remained far away from the higher education. This made

Ambedkar establish the people's Education Society on 8 July 1945 and start Siddhartha College on 19 June 1946 at Bombay.

The establishment of Siddhartha College was not only a turning point in the social life of the socially and economically backward classes but also an epoch-making event in the social reconstruction of Indian society. It marked the beginning of a new era throwing open the portals of the university to the working class people, in general and weaker sections in particular.

It was felt by many that only such professors, who believed in the ideology of Ambedkar would be appointed in Siddhartha College. However, they were surprised when Ambedkar appointed Prof. A.B. Gajendragadkar, who was a renowned Sanskrit scholar as the first Principal of Siddharta College. Subsequently, talented and experienced teachers from Brahmin and other communities like Dr. V.S. Patankar, Dr. J.V. Deshpande, Dr. H.R. Karnik, Prof. Anant Kanekar, Prof. M.B. Chitnis, Prof. G.C.Saldhana and Prof. Frank D'Souza were taken to Sidhartha College en-bloc from the Khalsa College of Bombay.

Milind Mahavidyalaya

After four years of the establishment of Siddhartha College, Ambedkar turned his eyes to the most backward Marathwada region of the erstwhile Hyderabad state. He set up Milind Mahavidyalaya with the faculties of arts, science and commerce at Aurangabad in 1950 with a loan of Rs. ten lakhs from the Hyderabad government with the help of B. Ramakrishana Rao and Gopalrao Ekbote who were then Chief Minister and

Education Minister respectively of the state. The loan was subsequently written off.

The foundation stone of the building of Milind Mahavidyalaya was laid by Dr. Rajendra Prasad, the first President of free India, on 1 September 1951. While welcoming the President, Ambedkar in his speech said: "Coming as I do from the lowest order of the Hindu society, I know what is the value of education. The problem of raising the lower order deemed to be economic. This is a great mistake. The problem of raising the lower order in India is not to feed them, to clothe them and to make them serve the higher classes as the ancient ideal of this country. The problem of the lower order is to remove from them that inferiority complex which has stunted their growth and made them slaves to others, to create in them the consciousness of the significance of their lives for themselves and for the country, of which they have been cruelly robbed of the existing social order. Nothing can achieve this purpose except the spread of higher education. This is in my opinion panacea of our social troubles."

These views were earlier expressed by Ambedkar on 5 October 1927 in the Bombay legislative assembly, while speaking on the Bombay University Amendment Bill:

I had the good fortune of listening to the speech of Ambedkar. I had then just done matriculation. I had gone to the function out of curiosity to see Ambedkar and Rajendra Prasad, at least from a long distance.

Marathwada was the most neglected region of the Nizam state in every respect and more so in education. There was only one college at Aurangabd and that too up to intermediate only in all the five districts of Marathwada. After completing my intermediate, which was equivalent to the present XII standard, I had to take up a job as a primary school teacher.

Being the son of an impecunious school teacher, it was beyond my reach to go to Hyderabad for further studies. The Milind Mahavidyalaya provided me a God-send opportunity to fulfil my ambition of becoming a graduate as the classes were conducted in the morning which I could attend while serving as a teacher.

The construction of the college building was in progress. Dr. Ambedkar used to come to Aurangabad to supervise and monitor the progress of the construction. In the evening, he used to sit in the easy chair in the open. I had an opportunity of seeing him from close and listening him talking to the persons. One day, I saw a group of persons coming to him in anxiety with Runjaji, who was probably his trusted attendant. They said: "Babasaheb, you have failed Shahare who is our boy and passed a Baman boy." I could not make out in the beginning but after hearing the whole conversation, I understood that Shahare who was a Mahar was not selected for the post of lecturer in Botany. Instead Khare, who was a Brahmin, was selected.

The reply Babasaheb gave to the group still rings in my ears. He told the group: "I have to build the generations here and the best teachers will only be appointed whatever the caste they belong to. Ask Shahare to prepare hard and come for the interview next year." Shahare was appointed as lecturer in Botany after one year. This is the same M.L. Shahare, who later rose to the position of a member of the Maharashtra Public Service Commission and a member of the Union Public Service Commission. But he could not become the Chairman of the People's Education Society in spite of his keen desire and frantic efforts, because of group politics.

That was Dr. Ambedkar. He never made compromise on the appointment of teachers. He had once said: "I would employ the most orthodox Brahmin, if he can make my students better than himself."

Ambedkar chose M.B. Chitnis, who was a Saraswat Brahmin, to be the first Principal of Milind Mahavidyalaya. The teachers who taught us were from different communities. I recollect a few names such as Dr. K.A. Thakar, Dr. Khare, B.D. Mahajan, Pinge, Naravane, Ransumbhe, Murli Hali, M.N. Wankhede, N.P. Sharma, R.S. Gupte, Agni, Mrs Patil.

I have had the privilege of knowing M.B. Chitnis intimately for two reasons. One, his naughty son was in my school. Second, my keen desire to do B.A. brought his patronage to me.

I have seen and known from close quarters as to how Chitnis set up and developed the college in fierce opposition of the diehards from Marathwada who could not relish the idea of running a college by Ambedkar. They directly or indirectly created hurdles in the way of Chitnis.

To cut the long story short, I obtained the degree of B.A. in the year 1955. Milind Mahavidyalaya indeed opened doors for me to obtain later B.Ed. and M.A. degrees. But for Ambedkar I would not have fulfilled my intense desire of becoming a graduate and a postgraduate. I pay my homage to the memory of Dr. Babasaheb Ambedkar.

Marathwada University

It was again the foresight and vision of Ambedkar that brought Marathwada University into existence in 1958.

Marathwada has been known for many centuries as a region of great cultural and historical importance. It can well be described as the home of art, religion and literature. The caves of Ajanta and Ellora which lie in this region and attract scholars, artists, students of religion and other visitors from distant parts of the world every year, furnish evidence of the great heights that were reached in painting, sculpture and architecture by the anonymous artists, craftsmen and builders of India who in ancient times dedicated their lives and their art to the glorification of the three great religions of India: Buddhism, Hinduism and Jainism. It was here that the glorious spiritual and literary traditions that have earned for Marathwada the title of the *land of saints* and the epithet of the cradle of *Marathi literature*, were built up by great poet-saints, philosophers and religious leaders like Dnyaneshwar, Eknath and Ramdas, whose lasting contributions to Marathi have made it one of the richest of modern Indian literatures. Here, too, are interred the mortal remains of Guru Gobind Singh and of many Sufi saints. Siraj, a great poet of early Urdu literature, and Wali, known as the father of modern Urdu poetry, were both born and lived here, in the city of Aurangabad. Paithan, formerly known as Prathisthan, the capital of Satavahana Empire and Daulatabad, or Deogiri, as it was called in earlier times when it was the capital of Yadava kings, are places of historic fame sought out by scholars of history.

The frescos of the caves of Ajanta and the sculptures that adorn these caves as well as those of Ellora, not to mention the Aurangabad caves, which have come into prominence at a more recent date, contain treasures of art valued not merely for their intrinsic merit as works of art but also for their religious and historical importance. They have furnished models and materials for study to generations of professional and amateur artists and lovers of art, and have been perennial source of inspiration to artists and students of art in this country and many foreign lands. Students of religion and philosophy, historians and sociologists, too, have drawn liberally upon these treasures for their own specialized studies. They also provide a true picture of the conditions, the mode of life, the habits, manners, styles of dress and adornment of the human figure and the ideas of the people of India, in short, in periods contemporaneous with the lives of the artists.

Marathwada holds the pride of place in the whole of Maharashtra for its wealth of religious, philosophical and poetical literature. Mukundraj, the first Marathi poet, was a son of the soil. He belonged to Nath Panth, a popular religious sect, interested in social reform. He was the author of *Vivekasindhu*, a work written in A.D. 1188, with the object of bringing the substance of the *Vedas* within the reach of those who were denied the benefit of their study by reason of birth in one of the non-privileged castes. Dnyaneshwar, often described as the father of Marathi literature on account of the superb quality of his writings and the influence they had on subsequent Marathi literature, and renowned as the author of *Dnyaneshwari*, an unrivalled commentary on the *Bhagavad Gita*, was the pioneer of the *Varkari Pantha*. The members of this sect, which was in the vanguard of the liberal movements based on the principles of equality and fraternity that flourished in the twelfth and thirteenth centuries, tried to spread their message to the lower strata of society through Marathi. The early Marathi poets happened to belong to the lowest castes, based on the occupations they followed. Thus, Namdev was a tailor, Gora Kumbhar, a potter, Zoga Permanand, an oilman, Savata Mali, a gardener, and Chokha Mela, a Mahar.

Chakradhar, a Gujrati saint, founded what came to be known as the Mahanubhava cult, based on the worship of Bhagwan Sri Krishna, which later spread as far as the Punjab. The followers of Chakradhar who belonged to Marathwada made valuable contribution to Marathi literature through a secret code of language known only to the initiated. Some of their writings have been deciphered and made available in the ordinary Marathi script by scholars of the twentieth century. Mahendrabhat, the first prose writer in Marathi and compiler of Chakradhar's sayings, belonged to Marathwada. So did the great Mahanubhava poets, Narendra, Damodhar and Bhaskar Bhatt.

Eknath, another great poet-saint, was born in Paithan in A.D. 1548. His *Bhagwata* is regarded as second only to the *Dnyaneshwari*. He led the renaissance in Marathi literature in the sixteenth century, and was a redoubtable champion of the untouchables. His contemporary, Dasopant, was also a well-known writer. Mukteshwar, the grandson of Eknath, another Marathi writer, was born in Paithan in A.D. 1609. Ramdas, founder of the *Ramdasi Pantha,* also belonged to the Marathwada region. All these writers from Marathwada were moved by a social urge to convey the message of religion to the common people in their own language, namely, Marathi, which they could easily understand.

Three towns were suggested for the location of the university, namely, Aurangabad, Nanded and Mominabad. Aurangabad was finally chosen as the most suitable place for the seat of the university from several points of view. The chief reasons were its importance as the cultural centre of Marathwada, apart from its being the administrative headquarters of the Marathwada division, its great historical traditions, its importance as a tourist center and its salubrious climate.

In Aurangabad, three sites were suggested for the establishment of the university. One near Chikalthana, a second starting from the boundary of Milind Mahavidyalaya and sloping down to Soneri Mahal at the foot of the hills, and a third near Padegaon on Daulatabad road.

The first two sites were rejected and Soneri Mahal site was selected as it was much bigger in area (670 acres) with the hills in the background. The Soneri Mahal site had the further advantage of being in the proximity of the Milind Mahavidyalaya. Dr. Ambedkar had visualized that as and when the university came it would be located in the Soneri Mahal area and therefore he had set up his Milind Mahavidyalaya where it is today.

The first two Vice Chancellors of the university, namely S.R. Dongerkerry and Dr. N.R. Tawda strictly followed Dr. Babasaheb Ambedkar in the appointment of teachers in the university. Both Dongerkerry and Tawde believed that that a university that is content to have second-rate teachers on its staff will always remain a second-rate university. So they were determined, even at the risk of being unpopular, that so long they were Vice Chancellors no one should be appointed as a university teacher if he did not come up to the required standard. After their retirement, subjective considerations seemed to have dominated the appointment of teachers.

Principal M.B. Chitnis was appointed as the first Registrar.

My career took strides, i.e., from a teacher to a Social Education Officer, from the Social Education Officer to a District Publicity Officer and then to Assistant Registrar in Marathwada University.

I joined Marathwada University in 1966 as Assistant Registrar, while Chitnis was still the Registrar. I had the good fortune of shaping myself as university administrator under the able guidance of M.B. Chitnis. After the retirement of Chitnis, I held the posts of Deputy Registrar, Controller of Examinations, Development Officer and Registrar during 24 years of my service in the university. When the University became the den of politics and centre of academic fraud, I preferred to proceed on voluntary retirement in 1990 with the determination to spend the rest of my life in reading and writing books.

I closely observed the working of the affiliated colleges including People's Education Society's colleges at Aurangabd.

I find a vast difference between the working of the colleges then and now.

Ambedkar had said: "The People's Education Society's objective is not merely to give education, but to give education in such a manner as to promote intellectual, moral and social democracy. This is what modern India needs and this is what all well wishers of India must promote."

Ambedkar expected that in an academic institution, the teachers and the taught would meet the challenges of the modern world by acquisition as well as application of knowledge. He held that professors should constantly acquire knowledge and seek the truth and practise it. He wanted universities to be sacred abodes of learning and not to be workshops for training an army of clerks.

If we dispassionately cast an eye on the teachers of the universities and the colleges, one can without fear of contradiction say that they are far away from the expectations of Ambedkar. The universities seem to have become the cafeterias to provide junk food rather than the sacred abodes of learning. The teachers seem to be interested more in academic fraud rather than academic excellence.

9

Failure of Scheduled Castes Leadership

Every scheduled caste leader taking a cue from Ambedkar repeatedly pronounced at public meetings in general and during election campaign in particular that the scheduled castes should be the governing class in India.

Ambedkar himself had said: "I have not been able to fulfil my life's ambition. I wanted to see my people a governing class in my lifetime sharing the political power in terms of equality with other communities."

The scheduled castes leaders, unfortunately have neither been able to fulfil Ambedkar's ambition nor have they been able to capture power so far on their own strength.

Division of Mahars and non-Mahars

The first and foremost reason is the internal divisions between the Mahars and the non-Mahars. The Mahars in Maharashtra were the first among the untouchables to take advantage of all the opportunities created by the British rule and even earlier by the East India Company. They used these opportunities to liberate themselves from the shackles of the 'Watan' and 'Baluta' system. They also took to education, began creating an organization for self-reform and in the process, they became conscious of their political and social rights. The Mahars, under the leadership of Ambedkar, launched the movement of the untouchables in Maharashtra to demand political consessions. This made the Chambhars, Maangs, Dhors and Bhangis suspicious that Ambedkar would not do anything for them. And as the Congress Party moved to mobilize the untouchables, it was natural for these castes and sub-castes to turn to the Congress Party rather than to the movement led by Ambedkar. This divide was further reinforced when the Mahars embraced Buddhism.

This division between the Mahars and the non-Mahars was further reinforced because of the prevalence of the notion of pollution in the untouchables too. For example, the Chambhars considered themselves more pure than either the Maangs or Mahaars. Similarly, the Maangs and Mahars also considered each other to be superior. The ritual differences among these three communities were paralleled by socioeconomic differences as well. The Chambhars were economically more secure, even today, than either the Maangs or the Mahars. But they were not fortunate to produce a leader of Ambedkar's stature. Jagjivan Ram, of course emerged but he could not reach the height of Ambedkar. However he kept himself in power until he breathed his last. He missed the Prime Ministership by inches because he was a Chambhar. I was told by a reliable source that the Janata Party on the advice of Jayaprakash Narayan had come to the decision that their Government should be headed by Jagjivan Ram. But those who were against him for his being Chambhar sent Rajnarayan to Chaudhari Charan Singh. He inflated the ego of the Jaat by saying that a Chambhar is going to become the Prime Minister and he will have to work under him. Charan Singh immediately rushed to Jayaprakash Narayan and told him that under no circumstances he will agree to Jaggu (Jagjivan Ram) to become Prime Minister. As a result Morarji Desai was installed as Prime Minister.

Ambedkar's movement failed to mobilize the non-Mahar untouchable castes on the one hand and develop a close ideological relationship with the non-Brahmin Bahujan Samaj on the other hand. As such it posed a great hurdle in the development of a unified political force. The other was Ambedkar's failure to transform the caste movement to a class movement

Ambedkar did not try to unite the Bahishkrut Samaj with the Shramik or the workers employed in different mills and trades. He did advocate the necessity of building a socialist society as an appropriate system for the uplift of the down trodden. However, he did not hesitate to give vent to his contempt for Marx and Marxists. It is not, therefore, surprising to find Kuber observing: "It is inconceivable how he (Ambedkar) could achieve socialism by repudiating Marxism and making Buddhism an alternative to Marxism. The miseries of the world must be eradicated by material methods. And they cannot be removed only by a change of religion."

Unfortunately, the scheduled castes could not develop into powerful political force both inside the central and state legislatures and within the party to which they belonged. The various Republican Party of India splinter groups are hopelessly marginalized in terms of electoral strength. The legislators are again hopelessly divided into many parties without any cooperation whatsoever on issues of vital importance to the society.

Lok Sabha debates 1962 to 1971 show that despite the sizeable number of scheduled castes members among the central legislature very few of them participated in the debates, even those related to the problems of the scheduled castes. The making of laws for the welfare of the scheduled castes has generally been a slow process in spite of the fact that some of the major problems for long have been identified. Some of the measures proposed in the Lok Sabha during the period under review were either withdrawn or were inconclusive, or were not rigorously pursued. The discussion on the reports of the Commissioner for Scheduled Castes and Scheduled Tribes were more or less ritualistic. Some of the reports were not discussed at all. The Scheduled Castes and Scheduled Tribes Order (Amendment) Bill introduced in 1967 was passed during the emergency. Similarly, the Amendment to the untouchability Offence Act remained inconclusive for nearly 16 years. (G. Narayan, *Rule Making for Scheduled Castes in Lok Sabha*, pp. 433-40)

There is another interesting study by Satish Saberwal on reserved constituency candidates and consequences, which concludes that the scheduled castes leaders tend to use their political base for personal gains. None among them understands the larger institutional mechanism which underlies and renewed current inequalities, nor do any have the stamina for applying themselves to the task of changing the larger system so that its processes would generate effective social, economic and political equality. (*Reserved Constituency, Candidates and Consequences*, Saberwal Satish, p. 71)

This shows that scheduled castes legislators failed to develop an effective bargaining power as envisaged by Ambedkar to check the political power of the dominant non-scheduled castes ruling political parties.

It has become customary on the part of the scheduled castes legislators to accept the portfolio of social Welfare, while Ambedkar considered Finance, Home, Revenue and Industries as the most important portfolios and the rest of the portfolios, he considered as secondary.

The scheduled castes leaders failed to realize that their marginalization on various issues in the legislature was restricted by the effective centres of power which are located beneath the formal decision-making structures. On the contrary the personnel of the ruling class controlled the key decisions, and the influence of scheduled castes and subordinate classes has remained quite negligible on the issue of vital importance to scheduled castes.

The scheduled castes leaders do not seem to have understood that the political power of the dominant classes is based on an unstable equilibrium of compromise. The ruling class in India conceded from time to time scheduled castes, demands which are comparatively innocuous, and hence do not challenge the capitalist structure. In this connection it is interesting to note that despite the opposition to Article 31, Ambedkar had to approve its incorporation as a Fundamental Right in the Constitution of India.

This is what Ambedkar said about Article 31 in Parliament on 19 March 1955:

"Article 31 is an article for which I and the Drafting Committee can take no responsibility whatsoever. We do not take any responsibility for that. That is not our draft. The reason was that the Congress Party, at that time when Article 31 was being framed was so divided within itself that we did not know what to do, what to put and what not to put. There were three sections in the Congress Party. One section was led by Sardar Vallabbhai Patel, who stood for all compensation, full compensation in the sense in which full compensation is enacted in our Land Acquisition Act, namely, market price plus 15 per cent solatium. That was his point of view. Our Prime Minister was against compensation. Our friend, Mr. Pant, had conceived his Zamindari Abolition Bill before the Constitution was being actually framed. He wanted a very safe delivery for his baby. So he had his own proposition. There was thus the tripartite struggle, and we left the matter to them to decide in any way they liked. And they merely embodied what their decision was in Article 31."

Ambedkar further said: "This Article 31, in my judgement, is a very ugly thing. Something which I do not like to look at."

The following dialogue took place between Ambedkar and Mulk Raj Anand in May 1950 on Fundamental Rights:

MRA: As a member of the Constituent Assembly have you been able to assert the rights of the individual? I see that your committee gives fundamental rights... the right of the individual to freedom. But we see that you have also conceded the right to property as fundamental right... Does not the right to property give a decisive advantage to those who have inherited wealth? So the poorest of the poor, the untouchables, will always be at a disadvantage.

BRA: In our Constitution, we have put forward the ideal of a secular, socialist democracy... If everyone can have the right to till the land from the state tenancy rights then equality of privilege can be assured, and there need be no exploitation. So far, untouchables and even many caste Hindus and Muslims do not have tenancy rights. All these landless peasants are mere hands.

MRA: Then the right to work should have been recognized as a fundamental right.

BRA: I was the only one of the members of the drafting committee.

MRA: So you became a lamb before the lions!

BRA: I bleated a good deal! I am now roaring!

MRA: As a lawyer, you know how the judges will always decide in favour of the high caste and upper class Hindus.

BRA: Of course, the only non-Brahmin in our government of pundits, Jawaharlal Nehru fought hard against the right to own property being a fundamental right... But Babu Rajendra Prasad felt that Nehru wanted to make India into Russia. The caste Hindus therefore only conceded the other rights of man as directive principles... to be fought for in Parliament.

MRA: Which would be weighed in favour of men of property?

BRA: The socialists can win a majority one day. And ask for redress. Anyhow, the outcastes and tribals have been declared scheduled castes. They will be given certain privileges to uplift them like reservation for admission to schools and colleges and scholarships.

MRA: The caste Hindus will always resent reservation.

BRA: We must organize ourselves. Arouse the disinherited to fight. There are more outcastes than caste Hindus—if we include the Muslims who are also regarded as untouchables by the casteists and the tribal people. Together with the socialists they can abolish ownership of private property! No, landlords, no tenants! No landless labourers!

MRA: State capitalism might also prove to be dangerous. You know what Stalin has done in Russia? Imposed a set of bureaucrats on the people in the name of communism.

BRA: Of course, we must protect the individual from invasion of his rights from other individuals. Liberty of the person must always be a primary concern. That was in my mind when I urged for fundamental rights.

MRA: If that was in your mind then you might urge parliament to revise fundamental rights. We must fight against both state capitalism and private capitalism. You know how the vast majority of people everywhere are subject to the will of the employers.

BRA: Indeed, liberty so far seems to be the liberty of the landlord to increase rent. The capitalists always want to reduce wages and increase hours of work.. .capitalism is a dictatorship of private employer.

MRA: The fundamental rights—right to life, liberty and happiness—remain a dream.

Scheduled castes leaders by and large have not been able to use State power for any serious attack on the existing social order in any of its main or subsidiary features because their very entrance in the legislature is dependent on the dominant socioeconomic forces of the reserved constituencies from which they are elected. Their candidature is sponsored by this Congress or that Congress. And this sponsored mobility in return demands not assertiveness and protest but subservient to party bosses inside the legislatures.

Ambedkar himself had realized the limits of his own concept of political power to be pursued within the parameters of democracy. He experienced the supersession and alienation of scheduled castes voice in parliament itself. For example, he could not get the Hindu Code Bill passed. He was disgusted with the delaying tactics adopted by the orthodox sections in the ruling party which prevented the passing of the Hindu Code Bill. Prime Minister Nehru wavered because of political pressures from within the party and thought that it was desirable to get a part of it enacted into law rather than allow the whole of it go waste. Ambedkar reluctantly agreed to move the Bill in its truncated form. After a couple of days, Nehru told Ambedkar to drop the Bill, even the marriage and divorce portion of the Bill that was under discussion. Thus, the Hindu Code Bill, the greatest social reform measure ever undertaken by the legislature in this country, was killed and it died unwept and unsung after four clauses of it were passed.

Ambedkar thus let down and fully frustrated in his last attempt to improve the Hindus relinquished his post of the Law Minister.

On the eve of general elections for the first Lok Sabha, Ambedkar during his election campaign had said: "In the Parliament, there are 30 untouchable members belonging to the Congress party. I ask them, have they done anything for our people? They never asked any questions; they never moved any resolution; and they never submitted any Bill in the Parliament, because their voice is suppressed by the Congress."

Thus, though Ambedkar earlier seems to be insisting on the need of sending sincere and committed scheduled castes members to the parliament, he was subconsciously aware of the ineffectiveness of these scheduled castes members in the parliament. Probably, because of this, the committee presided over by Ambedkar in 1955 at Bombay passed a resolution expressing the need to abolish political reservation in central and state legislatures and at the local self bodies and at the district level.(C.D. Khairmode, *Bhimrao Ramji Ambedkar*, Vol. II, p. 179)

In his speech at Agra on 18 March 1956, Ambedkar had said: "Today's reservation in services is not going to exist for ever all times to come. Buddhism will then show us the right path on our becoming Buddhists. We will have the opportunities to be equal partners in all walks of life. The Buddhist countries will also come to our rescue and raise our voice." (Nanak Chand Rattu, *Last Few Years of Dr. Ambedkar*, p. 74)

Speaking in the Lok Sabha on 6 December 1956, N.V. Gadgil, who was then a minister in the central cabinet, said: "Very recently I had some discussion with Dr. Ambedkar and he said to me, 'No more previleges to the scheduled castes. Now they must come into their own and fight against injustice that is still there alongwith the rest of the members of the whole Indian community.' (*Writings and Speeches of Dr. Babasaheb Ambedkar,* Vol. 15, p. 982)

The thinking of Ambedkar on the above lines was probably because of his disillusion from his followers in general and educated class in particular. Had he remained alive, I think, he would have not pressed for the extension in the period of reservation.

In his speech on 28 September 1956, at Bombay, Ambedkar had said that he had lost faith in the educated men of his community and pinned his faith on the illiterates. (Dhananjay Keer, *Dr. Babasaheb Ambedkar-Life and Mission:* Popular Prakashan, Mumbai, p. 444)

10

Fate of Buddhism in India

Swami Vivekananda was the first to recognize and publicly declare the Hindu indebtedness to Buddha's ideas. He saw the inseparable bond between Buddhism, Vedanta and Vaishnavism. He eulogized the Buddha and the Vedanta; he laughed at the puerile myths built by the Brahmins around Buddha as an Avatar. He used strong words to denounce the ancient Brahmins for their intolerance and selfishness. He recognized the institution of monks with a view to training them for *bahujan hitaya*, for the happiness and good of all.

Vivekananda was an insightful visionary. He constructed a grand vision and a beautiful harmonious and synthetic picture of Indian philosophy and storiology. He visualized the serene and majestic figure of the Buddha established at the centre of the multi-structured, multifaceted, and multi-coloured citadel of 'Hinduism,' illuminating the entire universe with His unique wisdom and radiating His profound loving kindness in all directions. Therefore, "I prostrate before the Lord Buddha," Vivekananda exclaimed in devout and conscious enthusiasm. The other Brahminical and Hinduistic teachers and leaders before Him had merely plundered the metaphysical and spiritual wealth of the Thatagata; and in place of gratitude, they had given him a few names, such as an out-caste, a nihilist, a barbarian and a leader and teacher of demons! It was Swami Vivekananda, who sincerely and devoutly affirmed: "The Lord is my Ishta—my God. He preached no theory about Godhead—He was himself a God. I fully believe it. (*Complete Works of Vivekananda,* Vol. VI, p. 27)

The attitude of Swami Vivekananda to Buddhism is thus radically different from those of ancient and medieval followers of Hinduism. Vivekananda is grateful to Buddha and recognizes his debt to Buddha's legacy. He honours Buddha as the greatest teacher of Hinduism, as the greatest seer, the ideal karmayogin, the real vadantin, the only God that ever walked on earth.

In his speeches in Europe and United States of America, Swami Vivekananda freely praised Buddha and stressed on his ethical, rational and humanistic teachings. (Lal Mani Joshi, *Discerning the Buddha,* pp. XIX-XXI)

In modern times, Swami Vivekananda was perhaps, the first great Indian who reminded his countrymen as well as the Europeans and Americans of the greatness of the Buddha. The Buddhists all the world over will remain grateful to this great modern Hindu monk and leader for his contribution to spreading the knowledge about the Buddha and his teachings, especially in India where his very name had been nearly forgotten for many centuries.

Swami Vivekananda spoke of the greatness of Buddha so enthusiastically as to make the American audience feel that he was himself a Buddhist monk and a learned Buddhist preacher.

In so far as his love, admiration and reverence for Buddha are concerned, Swami Vivekananda is unequalled among non-Buddhists. No other Hindu has praised Buddha so consistently and wholeheartedly as he has done. It can be said without fear of contradiction, that not even the most earnest and devout among the modern Buddhists have displaced so much zeal and generosity in honouring the Thatagata with beautiful flowers of moving speech as is found in the lectures, epistles and books of Swami Vivekananda.

Swami Vivekananda said: "The Great Man, the Man among men, the Buddha, was born in India six centuries before Christ. He is one of the most historical prophets of the world. The Buddha and Mohammad are the two most historical persons, and the Buddha is the most ancient historical teacher. Krishna is very mythological." (Lal Mani Joshi, *Discerning the Buddha*, p. 55)

In one of his lectures in America, Swami Vivekananda said: "...You remember that passage of the sermon of Buddha, how He sent a thought of love towards the south, the north, the east and the west, above and below, until the whole universe was filled with love, so grand, great, and infinite." This statement corresponds to a verse in the *Mettasutta*, Discourse on Loving Kindness, of the Pali *Sattanipata*, which I quote below:

"Just a mother would protect her only child even at the risk of her own life, even so let a man cultivate boundless heart towards all beings. Let his thought of infinite love pervade the whole universe, above, below and across, without any obstruction, without any hatred, without any enmity." The same teaching of Buddha is expressed in beautiful and memorable words by Paul Carus thus:

Do not deceive, do not despise
Each other, anywhere.
Do not be angry, nor should ye
Secret resentment bear;
For as a mother risks her life
And watches over her child,
So boundless be your love to all,
So tender, kind and mild.
Yea, cherish good-will right and left,
All round, early and late,
And without hindrance, without
stint,
From every free and hate,
While standing, walking, sitting
down,
Whatever you have in mind,
The rule of life that is always best
Is to be loving kind.

Buddha seems to have been the only prophet who did everything for others and absolutely nothing for himself. He gave up his home and all the enjoyments of life to spend his days in search of the medicine for the terrible disease of human misery. The way to ultimate peace and bliss which he had discovered constitutes the Buddhist medicine against all the ills of existence. An ancient *Mahayanasutra* describes Buddha as the King of Physicians (*Vaidyaraja*) and as the Dispenser of immortal medicine (*smrtabhesaja-pradah*). Chandrakirti, the philosopher (7th century), calls Him the Great King of Doctors, the Physician of the great disease of passions (*klesa-mahavyadhi-cikitsaka-mahavaidya-raja*).

Buddha is revered as the Torchbearer of Mankind in the *Suttanipata*. He attained Illumination (*bodhi*) and diffused it all over the world; that Spiritual Torch emitted a Light that dispelled the darkness not only of men but also of Gods. The Buddhists rever Him as the Teacher of gods and men. The word 'Buddha' symbolizes light, awakening, enlightenment, knowledge and wisdom. It also symbolizes moral perfection and spiritual fulfilment. Buddha is thus the source of wisdom and morality and of all those good qualities of head and heart that civilized humanity cherishes and cultivates. Swami Vivekananda repeatedly stresses these qualities of Buddha's character.

Swami Vivekananda has fully grasped the greatness of Buddha as the Torchbearer of mankind in this world of darkness. He said: "That man set in motion the highest moral ideas any nation can have. Whenever there is a moral code, it is ray of light from the Man." (Lal Mani Joshi, *Discerning the Buddha,* p. 59)

Swami Vivekananda was the first Hindu in the modern times to say repeatedly: "Buddha was the first to teach universal brotherhood of man. It is a cardinal principle of the Buddhist faith today. Selfishness, egoism, casteism and unequality are the curses of mankind. Buddha was the first to find out these curses. He was the first to make a diagnosis of these terrible diseases of humanity. His way of universal liberation was open to all human beings. Buddha was thus the supreme benefactor of humanity. He worked for the benefit of others and taught the supreme principle of selfless service to others. I therefore, prostrate myself before Lord Buddha."

A few months after the Enlightenment, Buddha commanded his first sixty disciples as follows:

"Go ye forth, monks, and wander, for the spiritual well beings of the many, for the spiritual happiness of the many, out of compassion for the world beings, for the good, for the well being and for the happiness of human and divine beings." Swami Vivekananda wanted this to be the ideal of the followers of the non-dual Vedanta. He firmly believed that until Buddha's heart comes once more in India, the people of India will remain in a hopeless state. He said: "I wish I had one infinitesimal part of Buddha's heart."

Swami Vivekananda also said: "It is my particular fancy that the same Buddha became Christ. Buddha prophesied, 'I will come again in 500 years' and Christ came here in 500 years. These are the two Lights of the whole human nature. Two men have been produced, Buddha and the Christ; these are the two giants, huge gigantic personalities, two Gods. Between them they divide the whole world. Wherever there is the least knowledge in the world, people bow down either to Buddha or Christ."

Swami Vivekananda occasionally quoted from the Buddhist (Pali) texts what he considered to be Buddha's words. Some of them are given below:

"What you think, that you are; what you think, that you will be."

"All that we are is the result of what we have thought; it is founded on our thoughts, it is made up of our thoughts. If a man speaks or acts with an evil thought, pain follows him, as the wheel follows the foot of the ox that draws the carriage. If a man speaks or acts with a pure thought, happiness follows him, like a shadow that never leaves him."

"Take care, for everything in the world is evanescent, and there is always misery in this life."

"Be an island unto yourself; take refuge in yourself, take no other refuge. You must accomplish your liberation through careful perseverance."

According to Swami Vivekananda, Buddha's religion consisted of three discoveries: the existence of evil; the cause of evil which lay in desire and selfishness; the cure of evil which was possible by becoming unselfish. Here he is obviously referring to the famous holy truths which are four. Suffering (*dukha*), the origin of suffering, the end of suffering, and the path leading to the end of suffering.

"Force cannot cure the evil of selfishness. Dirt cannot wash dirt; hate cannot cure hate." Here Swami Vivekananda is obviously summing up a verse of the *Dhammapada* which may be rendered thus: "Never does hatred cease by hatred; it ceases by friendliness; this is the ancient rule (Dharma)."

Swami Vivekananda visited Bodh Gaya twice, first at the beginning of his missionary career, and again at the end of his life, on the morning of his 39th birthday. Sitting under the holy Bodhi Tree, he is said to have asked himself: "Is it possible that I breathe the air He breathes? That I touch the earth He trod?" At some stage during his tours in India, he is said to have been permitted to touch the sacred relics of Buddha.

An important element in Swami Vivekananda's interpretation of Buddhism is that the Buddhists misunderstood and misinterpreted the teachings of Buddha. He said: "Our views about Buddha are that he was not understood properly by his disciples; it was his own followers who did not realize the import of his teachings. The error of misunderstanding consisted chiefly in not seeing the truth that Buddha's teachings were the fulfillment of the truths of the Hindu religion."

Dr. S. Radhakrishnan in his *Indian Philosophy* says: " Buddha did not feel that he was announcing a new religion. He was born, grew up, and died a Hindu. He was relating with a new emphasis the ancient ideals of the Indo-Aryan civilization. Buddhism did not start as a new and independent religion. It was an offshoot of the more ancient faith of the Hindus, perhaps a schism or heresy. While on the fundamentals of metaphysics and ethics, Buddha agreed with the faith, he inherited, he protested against certain practices which were in vogue at the time. He refused to acquiesce in the Vedic ceremonialism. Buddha's main object was to bring about a reformation in religious practices and a return to the basic principles.

"Buddha utilized the Hindu inheritance to correct some of the expressions. He came to fulfil, not to destroy. For us, in this country, Buddha is an outstanding representative of our religious traditions. He left his footprints on the soil of India and his mark on the soul of the country with its habits and convictions. While the teaching of Buddha assumed distinctive forms in the other countries of the world in conformity with their traditions, here, in the home of Buddha, it has entered into and became an integral part of our culture. The *Brahamanas* and *Sarmanas* were treated alike by Buddha and the two traditions gradually blended. In a sense Buddha is a maker of modern Hinduism."

In *Dhammapad* Chapter 29, Brahmanavagga, Buddha himself, refuted the claim of four Brahmins and called himself a true Brahmin.

Radhakrishan found in Buddhism only a restatement of the thought of the *Upanishads* with a new emphasis. Referring to the silence about the set aside questions, he observed: "To me silence is not a proof of denial or agnosticism. Silence is on occasions the only language of true worship. Our thoughts of God are always images though they may not be graven images."

Radhakrishan further observes: "Among the inspiring treasures of the human spirit is the memory of Gautama the Buddha. Its hold over the imagination of millions of our fellow beings is immense; its inspiration to braver and nobler living for centuries is incalculable; its contribution to the refining of the spirit of man and the humanizing of his social relations is impressive." (S. Radhakrishnan, *Eastern Religion and Western Thought,* p. 330)

Radhakrishnan's views are further strengthened by Bharat Ratnawardee P.V. Kane. He says: "Buddha was only a great reformer of the Hindu religion as practised in his time. Buddha did not feel or claim that he was forming a new religion, nor did he renounce the Hindu religion and all its practices and beliefs. He referred to the *Vedas* and Hindu sages with honour in some of his sermons. He recognized the importance of Yogic practices and meditation. His teaching took over several beliefs current among the Hindus in his days such as the doctrine of karma and rebirth and cosmological theories. A substantial portion of the teaching of Buddha formed part of the tenets of the *Upanishadic* period. The central *Upanishaa* conception of the immanence of brahma is never attacked by Buddha or by the early propagators of Buddhism."

In support of the theory that Buddha continued the tradition of ancient Vedic and Brahmanic seers, Radhakrishnan and Kane have quoted a passage from the canonical text in the Pali, which is given below:

"Even so have I, O Bhikkhus, seen an ancient path, an ancient road, followed by rightly enlightened persons of former times. And what, O Bhikkhus, is that ancient path, that ancient road, followed by the rightly enlightened ones of former times? Just this very Noble Eightfold path....This, O Bhikkhus, is that ancient path, that ancient road, followed by the rightly enlightened ones of former times. Along that path I have gone and while going along that path, I have fully come to know old age and death....Having come to know it fully, I have told it to the monks, the nuns, the lay followers, men and women, this brahmacharya is prosperous, flourishing, widespread, widely known, has become popular, and made manifest well by gods and men." Commenting on this passage Kane remarks that Buddha does not claim that he was unique, but claimed that he was only one of a series of enlightened men and stressed that the moral qualities which he urged men to cultivate belonged to antiquity.

Rhys Davids says: "Gautama was born and brought up and lived and died as a Hindu. There was not much in the metaphysics and principles of Gautama which cannot be found in one or the other of the orthodox systems, and a great deal of his morality could be matched from earlier or later Hindu books. Such originality as Gautama possessed lay in the way in which he adapted, enlarged, ennobled, and systematized that which had already been well said by others; in the way in which he carried out to their logical conclusion principles of equity and justice already acknowledged by some of the most prominent Hindu thinkers. The difference between him and other teachers lay chiefly in his deep earnestness and in his broad public spirit of philanthropy." (Jawaharlal Nehru, *The Discovery of India*, pp. 177-78)

Jawaharlal Nehru, the first Prime Minister of India has drawn the following remarkable picture of Buddha's personality: "The conception of Buddha to which innumerable loving hands have given shape in carven stone and marble and bronze, seems to symbolize the whole spirit of Indian thought, or at least one vital aspect of it. Seated on the lotus flower, calm and impassive, above passion and desire, beyond the storm and strife of this world, so far away he seems, out of reach, unattainable. Yet again we look and behind those still, unmoving features there is a passion and an emotion, strange and more powerful than the passions and the emotions, we have known. His eyes are closed, but some power of the spirit looks out of them and a vital energy fills the frame. The ages roll by and Buddha seems not so far away after all, his voice whispers in our ears and tells us not to run away from the struggle but, calm-eyed, to face it, and to see in life ever great opportunities for growth and advancement.

"Personality counts today as ever, and a person who has impressed himself on the thoughts of mankind as Buddha has, so that even today there is something living and vibrant about the thought of him, must have been a wonderful man—a man who was, as Barth says, the finished model of calm and sweet majesty, of infinite tenderness for all that breathes and compassion for all that suffers, of perfect moral freedom, and exemption from every prejudice. And the nation and the race which can produce such a magnificent type must have deep reserves of wisdom and inner strength." (Jawaharlal Nehru, *The Discovery of India, p. 121*)

R.R.Diwakar in his biography of Bhagwan Buddha writes: "Today more than three hundred millions of Indians look upon Buddha as the ninth incarnation of Vishnu, the Supreme Lord. About 800 million Buddhists consider him to be the saviour, who through numerous transmigrations attained Buddhahood and showed people The Way. Thinkers and intellectuals all over the world are interested in Buddha as almost the first rationalist and democrat in matters spiritual and religious. It may be said that nearly half the world is attracted in one way or the other by Buddha and his teachings."

"But what is it," he continues, "that rouses to such a high pitch the interest of varied peoples in Buddha and his teachings?...It is not Buddhism so much, in its different religious forms, that attracts attention and exacts the homage of the non-Buddhist world, as the colossal spiritual and moral personality of Buddha and his simple teachings. It is the humanity of Buddha and the universality of his teaching that are the living fountain of interest for thinking and feeling humanity. Especially does his message of peace come to us as a soothing balm today in the atomic age, when the minds of all are distracted by the possible destructive use of nuclear weapons and fatal calamity that may in all likelihood, involve the world in utter ruin. Only the love of peace and humanity preached by Buddha can get the better passions raging in the human heart, and avert the tragedy. It is on account of these facts and the somewhat tragic circumstances of today that Buddha and his message have an added importance. Whatever Buddha thought and taught and did is of vital concern today, both for man's inner progress as well as for a happy and harmonious social life among the peoples of the world." (R.R.Diwakar, *Bhagwan Buddha, Bharatiya Vidya Bhavan,* pp. 1, 5, 6)

Shankaracharya admitted before Goenka Guruji that Buddha was not an avatar of Vishnu and that Hindus will not say so hereafter.

The famous Tamil poet Sittalai Sattanar has paid the following tribute to the Buddha:

> O Lord! You are the wise, the pure, the pious and the ancient, above all others in austerity.
>
> O Lord! You destroyed the evils and discarded anger; you are the Omniscient.
>
> O Lord! You conquered Mara; you are the Blissful; and you condemned the unholy and false ways.
>
> O Lord! Your feet are marked with the thousand spoked-wheels.
>
> I do not have thousand tongues!
>
> How shall I praise thee.

(Lal Mani Joshi, *Discerning the Buddha,* pp. 63-64)

Addressing the Buddha Jayanti meeting in Calcutta in 1925, Mahatma Gandhi said: "I do not for one moment consider that Buddhism has been banished from India. It is impossible to banish Buddha, that great Lord, Master and Teacher of mankind. So long as the world lasts, I have not a shadow of doubt that he will rank among the greatest of teachers of mankind."

Decline of Buddhism

The decline of vigour in the Order or the Sangha was a major cause of the decline of Buddhism. The vitality of the Sangha lay in the spirit of renunciation, self-discipline, broadmindedness, liberality, service and sacrifice for the many. When those characteristics weakened and were almost lost, the influence of the Order disappeared. Buddha himself, right up to the last days of his life, went on from one place to another inspiring and arousing the people and leading them to the noble path of righteousness. Sariputta, Mangollana and numerous other Arhant disciples of his followed the same ideals. As time went on, the Buddhist monks did their best to live up to those high principles and succeeded in converting a big part of the known world to the sublime doctrine of Buddha. In India, great kings and emperors embraced Buddhism and with zealous devotion worked for the preservation and spread of the Dhamma. By the eleventh century after Buddha there were great universities and centers for study throughout the country, some with as many as 10,000 students from every Buddhist land. Kings, nobles, merchants and the common people all contributed their share towards the maintenance of these institutions; but although these rich endowments and royal patronage made the Buddhist organizations strong and prosperous, they, at the same time, gradually undermined the high ideals of renunciation and sacrifice on which the Sangha and the universities were founded. The monks in course of time became used to an easy life devoted primarily to academic pursuits and religious celebrations; they grew lax and accepted perverse and worldly practices and beliefs which were contrary to the earlier ideals, and which hardly differed from those of the masses. This led to the disintegration of the Order into diverse sects, to the weakening of the moral standards of the Sangha, and to a corresponding waning of their influence on the people as well as to a gradual decline of the religious fervor, faith and devotion of the laity.

The Muslim invasion played an important part in the disappearance of Buddhism from India for, just when the Sangha began to decline in vigour, the Muslim invaders invaded the country, indiscriminately massacring the people and burning and destroying the shrines, monasteries and schools in their path. In the destruction of the University of Nalanda, it is recorded by Turkish historian Minhazad, in his book *Tavakata-i-Nasiri*, that thousands of monks were burned alive and yet more thousands beheaded, and the burning of the library continued for several months. With the destruction of the Sangha, the Buddhists were left without leaders, and Buddhism did not recover.

Another important factor in the decline of Buddhism in India was the strong opposition from the orthodox Hindu traditionalists. The orthodox members of the community had in their hearts always been against Buddhism, chiefly because of the loosening of their own hold on the masses. During the glorious days of Buddhism, under the protection of royal patronage, the sectarian Hindus could not raise their voice against Buddhism, but after its decline, the orthodox community was able to move without restraint and slowly converted Buddhist temples which had escaped destruction into Hindu temples; the Buddhists, lacking a strong leadership and subject to the surrounding community pressures, were slowly absorbed. In those parts of India which were not brought under the control of the Muslim invaders, the pressure of the caste system slowly brought about the end of Buddhism. (R.R.Diwakar, *Bhagwan Buddha, Bharatiya Vidya Bhavan,* pp.162-64)

Andre Malraux questioned Jawaharlal Nehru during one of his visits to Paris. "What was it that enabled Hinduism to push away organized Buddhism from India, without any major conflict, over a thousand years ago? How did Hinduism succeed in absorbing, as it were, a great and wide spread religion, without the usual wars of religion which disfigure the history of so many countries? What inner vitality or strength did Hinduism possess then which enabled it to perform this remarkable feat? And did India possess this inner vitality and strength today? If so, then her freedom and greatness were assured."

It was a question after Nehru's own heart, or rather the kind of question that his mind was frequently framing. But, he had no satisfactory answer to it for Malraux or for himself. However, Nehru in his *Discovery of India*, writes: "It is clear that there was no wide spread or violent extermination of Buddhism in India. Occasionally, there were local troubles or conflicts between a Hindu ruler and the Buddhist Sangha, or organization of Monks, which had grown powerful. These had usually a political origin and they did not make any essential difference."

Nehru further writes: "It must also be remembered that Hinduism was at no time wholly displaced by Buddhism. Even when Buddhism was at its height in India, Hinduism was widely prevalent. Buddhism died a natural death in India or rather it was a fading out and a transformation into something else."

Nehru continues: 'India,' says Keith, 'has a strange genius for converting what it borrows and assimilating it.' If that is true of borrowing from abroad or from alien sources, still more it is applicable to something that came out of its own mind and thought. Buddhism was not only entirely a product of India; its philosophy was in line with previous Indian thought and the philosophy of the *Vedanta* (the *Upanishads*). The *Upanishads* had even ridiculed present craft and ritualism and minimized the importance of the castes.

"Brahaminism made of Buddha an avatar, a god, so did Buddhism. Monasteries became rich, centres of vested interests, and their discipline became lax. Magic and superstition crept into the popular forms of worshiping. There was a progressive degeneration of Buddhism in India after the first millennium of its existence.

"Mrs. Rhys Davids points out its diseased state during that period: 'Under the overpowering influence of these sickly imaginations the moral teaching of Gautama have been almost hid from view. The theories grew and flourished, each new step, each new hypothesis demanded another; until the whole sky was filled with fragrances of the brain, and the nobler and simpler lessons of the founder of the religion were smothered beneath the glittering mass of metaphysical subtleties.' " (Jawaharlal Nehru, *The Discovery of India,* pp. 187-88)

Some degraded forms of Buddhism continued in East Bengal and in Sind in the north-west. Otherwise Buddhism gradually vanished from India as a widespread religion.

Nehru says: "Even in the long years of its decline in India, and when later it practically ceased to count as a separate religion, much of it remained as a part of the Hindu faith and in national ways of life and thought. Even though the religion as such was ultimately rejected by the people; the ineffaceable imprint of it remained and powerfully influenced the development of the race. This permanent effect had little to do with dogma or philosophic theory or religious belief. It was the ethical, social and practical idealism of Buddha and his religion that influenced people and left their imperishable mark upon them, even as the ethical ideals of Christianity affected Europe though it may not pay much attention to its dogmas, and as Islam's human, social, and practical approach influenced many people who were not attracted by its religious forms and beliefs." (Jawaharlal Nehru, *The Discovery of India,* p. 182)

Buddhism Today in India

The position of Buddhism in India is as explained by Vimalakitti in his editorial "Bauddha Samaj Kothe Aahe?" and in his article, "Audit of Ambedkar Movement" in the April-May 2010 issue of *Vijit Sangram.*

Ambedkar believed that the wave of conversion would spread and in a period of 15 years, India would become a Buddhist country and join the Buddhist world as a first rank revivalist of Buddhism in the land of its birth.

I venture to say that this belief remained a wishful thinking as the wave, instead of rising high, is on a progressive decline. If this is to be halted, the Buddhists in general and the followers of Ambedkar in particular will have to seriously study the editorial and article of Vimalakitti and devise remedies to keep Buddhism alive.

11

The Betrayal of Ambedkar

Ambitions of Ambedkar

Ambedkar had ambitions to set up a Buddhist university at Aurangabad, which is surrounded by sacred relics and monuments of the ancient Buddhist culture at Ajanta and Ellora.

He had also ambitions to set up a School of Political Thought for training those who cherished the desire to enter politics and join legislatures to shape the country.

Ambedkar did establish a School of Political Thought in Mumbai. He was sure of taking the school to greater height, gaining all-round reputation and popularity amongst the masses throughout the country. "The reputation," he said, "of such a school would depend greatly upon the ability and speaking capacity of the teachers."

He established the school with S.S. Rege as its Registrar and himself as its Founder and Director. In the initial stages, the school started with 15 students on its roll. However, with the deteriorating health and eyesight Ambedkar found it difficult to pay his much attention to the working of the school and chalk out the future programme for its development. As a result school breathed its last with him to the utter disappointment of the promising youths who wanted to carve their career in politics.

Ambedkar had the third ambition of setting up a Buddhist Seminary at Bangalore on a piece of land donated by the Maharaja of Mysore for the purpose of giving training to Bhikkhus and preachers of Buddhism.

But all three ambitions of Ambedkar remained on paper. The followers of Ambedkar could not bring any of these institutions into existence as conceived by Ambedkar.

Sad in Life

Dr. Ambedkar was sad in his personal as well as public life. His deteriorating health compelled him to marry Sharda Kabir much against the advice of his teacher Prof. P.V. Kane and his trusted lieutenant Gaikwad.

Ambedkar's first wife Ramabai was a devoted wife and spent days and nights in anxiety for her husband's safety and health, and she observed rigid fasts. On Saturdays she took only water and black gram, worshipped God and invoked his blessings on her husband.

Ambedkar's second wife was just the opposite of Ramabai in character and conduct. During Ambedkar's last days, it is well known that she made his life miserable. She seemed to have married him not to be his devoted wife but to enjoy life, taking advantage of his name, fame and position as expressed by Ambedkar himself.

Ambedkar felt dismayed and disappointed on both counts, namely, personal and public life.

On 29 July 1956, Nanak Chand Rattu, his Private Secretary, mustered his courage to ask his master: "Sir, why do you look so sad, worried and distressed these days, and even weep at times?"

Ambedkar brushed him aside, saying: "Go! Do your typing work and do not disturb me."

Nanak Chand sensed that there was something very serious which his master was trying to conceal. He repeated his question on 30 July 1956, with the determination of making his master reveal his mind. Ambedkar relented and with tears in his eyes told Nanak Chand: "You people do not know what is troubling me and what makes me so sad. The first worry to my mind is that I have not been able to fulfil my life's mission. I wanted to see my people a governing class in my life time sharing the political power in terms of equality with other communities. I am now almost crippled and prostrate with illness. Whatever I have been able to achieve is being enjoyed by the educated few, who, with their deceitful performances have proved to be a worthless lot, with no sympathies for their downtrodden brethren. They live for themselves, and their personal gains. Not one of them is prepared to do social work. They are treading the path of their ruination. I now wanted to divert my attention towards the vast illiterate masses in the villages, who continue to suffer and remained almost unchanged economically. But life seems short."

He continued: "I also wanted someone from the depressed classes to come forward in my life time and take the heavy responsibility of running the movement after me. There, however, seems none who would rise to the occasion. My lieutenants, in whom I had full faith and confidence to run the movement are fighting among themselves for leadership and power, unmindful of the heavy responsibility that is going to fall upon them."

Ambedkar further continued: "Anyhow I have done a lot in spite of the abuses hurdled at me from all sides and I will continue to do so till my death." So saying with tears rolling down his cheeks, he looked at Nanak Chand Rattu. After a little pause, wiping his tears, he said: "Tell my people, Nanak Chand, whatever I have done I have been able to do after passing through crushing miseries and endless troubles all my life fighting with my opponents." (Nanak Chand Rattu, *Last Few Years of Dr. Ambedkar*, pp. 93-94)

Ambedkar's agony proved prophetic. Shortly after his death conflicts and quarrels came to the surface among his lieutenants. They took cudgels in hand against each other for power and pelf. The party fragmented in various factions in quick succession.

Ambedkar's so-called followers in administration and politics used him as ladder to climb up and up, dashing the hopes and aspirations of their vast brethren to pieces. It would not be an exaggeration to say that they constitute as Brahmins among the untouchables. Most of them holding key positions, either in politics or bureaucracy, have married Brahmin girls who seem to have taken hold of them so much so that they are said to perform all the Hindu rituals which Ambedkar hated and discarded with contempt.

Ambedkar's last message conveyed through Nanak Chand Rattu was: "With great difficulty, I have brought this Caravan where it is seen today. Let the Caravan march on and further on despite the hurdles, pitfalls and difficulties that may come in its way. If my people, my lieutenants are not able to take the caravan ahead, they should leave it where it is seen today, but in no circumstances should they allow the Caravan to go back." (Nanak Chand Rattu, *Last Few Years of Dr. Ambedkar*, p. 94)

It is unfortunate that no scheduled caste leader of the calibre and stature of Ambedkar has emerged after his sad demise. As a result the Caravan, instead of marching ahead, has gone back. And the pendulum will keep on swinging back so long as the scheduled caste leadership continues to be in the hands of dwarfs and pygmies who join hands with this Congress or that Congress to cling to power.

It is interesting to note what Ambedkar had said about the untouchables, who joined the Congress. "The untouchables who are in the Congress are at the end of the tail and the tail so lengthened that it cannot wag. The representatives of the untouchables were supposed to be the watch dogs of untouchables, but they are muzzled dogs. Far from biting, they are not even able to bark."

Ambedkar had said this before independence. The position does not seem to have much after independence.

12

Beware of Ambedkar's Warnings

I have given below the views expressed by Dr. Babasaheb Amebdkar in the Constituent Assembly as Chairman of the Drafting Committee; in Parliament as the Law Minister; and in Rajya Sabha as its member. They revealed his knowledge, indepth study of the issues, fairlessness and courage of conviction. They also speak for his foresight and vision. They can, and should, in fact, be taken as his warnings in the interest of individuals, society and the nation on the whole to act before it becomes further late.

I begin with the Constituent Assembly.

Constituent Assembly

While introducing the Draft constitution in the Constituent Assembly on 4 November 1948, Ambedkar said: "The love of the intellectual Indians for the village community is of course infinite if not pathetic. It is largely due to the fulsome praise bestowed upon it by Metcalf who described them as little republic having nearly everything that they want within themselves, and almost independent of any foreign relations. The existence of these village communities, each one forming a separate little state itself has according to Metcalf, contributed more than any other cause to the preservation of the people of India, through all the revolutions and changes which they have suffered, and is in a high degree conducive to their happiness and to their enjoyment of a great portion of freedom and independence, no doubt the village communities have lasted where nothing else lasts.

"But those who take pride in the village communities do not care to consider what little part they have played in the affairs and the destiny of the country; and why? Their part in the destiny of the country has been well described by Metcalf himself who says: 'Dynasty after dynasty tumbles down. Revolution succeeds to revolution. Hindu, Pathan, Mughal, Maratha, Sikh, English are all masters in turn but the village communities remain the same. In times of trouble they arm and fortify themselves. A hostile army passes through the country. The village communities collect their cattle within their walls, and let the enemy pass unprovoked.'

"Such is the part the village communities have played in the history of their country. Knowing this, what pride can one feel in them? That they have survived through all vicissitudes may be a fact. But mere survival has no value. The question is on what plane they have survived. Surely on a low. Selfish level. I hold that these village republics have been ruination of India. I am therefore surprised that those who condemn provincialism and communalism should come forward as champions of the village. What is the village but a sink of localism, a den of ignorance, narrow-mindedness and communalism?

"The Draft Constitution is also criticized because of the safeguards it provides for minorities, in this, the Drafting

Committee has no responsibility. It follows the decision of the Constituent Assembly. Speaking for myself, I have no doubt that the Constituent Assembly has done wisely in providing such safeguards for minorities as it has done. In this country both the minorities and the majorities have followed a wrong path. It is wrong for the majority to deny the existence of minorities. A solution must be found which will serve a double purpose. It must recognize the existence of the minorities to, start with. It must also be such that it will enable majorities and minorities to merge someday into one. The solution proposed by Constituent Assembly is to be welcomed because it is a solution, which serves the twofold purpose.

"To diehards who have developed a kind of fanaticism against minority protection, I would like to say two things. One is that minorities are an explosive force which, if it erupts, can blow up the whole fabric of the state. The history of Europe bears ample and appalling testimony to this fact. The other is that the minorities in India have agreed to place their existence in the hands of majority. In the history of negotiations for preventing the partition of Ireland, Redmond said to Carson: 'Ask for any safeguards you like the Protestant minority but let us have a united Ireland.' Carson's reply was: 'Damn your safeguards, we don't want to be ruled by you.' No minority in India has taken this stand. They have loyally accepted the rule of the majority, which is basically a communal majority and not a political majority. It is for the majority to realize its duty not to discriminate against minority. Whether the minorities will continue or will vanish must depend upon this habit of the majority. The moment the majority loses the habit of discriminating against the minority, the minorities can have no ground to exist. They will vanish."

Ambedkar could see years ahead the wisdom behind the provisions regarding safeguards to the minorities.

While speaking in the Constituent Assembly on 25 November 1949, he said: "I feel, however, good a Constitution may be, it is sure to turn out bad Constitution. May be, it may turn out to be good if those who are called to work it happen to be a good lot. The working of the Constitution does not depend only upon the nature of the Constitution. The Constitution can provide only the organs of the state such as the legislature, the executive and the judiciary. The factors on which the working of these organs of the State depends are the people and the political parties they will set up as their instruments to carry out their wishes and their policies. Who can say how the people of India and their parties will behave? Will they uphold the Constitutional methods of achieving their purposes or will they prefer revolutionary methods, however good a Constitution may be? It is, therefore, futile to pass any judgment upon the Constitution without reference to the part which the people and their parties are likely to play."

Dr. Ambedkar believed that "Social and economic democracy are the tissues and fibres of political democracy." He warned that "to leave equality between class and class, between sex and sex which is the soul of Hindu society untouched and to go on passing legislation relating to economic problem is to make a farce of our Constitution and to build a palace on a dung-heap."

In his speech after the adoption of the Constitution by the Constituent Assembly on 26 November 1949, Ambedkar said: "The task of the Drafting Committee would have been a very difficult one if this Constituent Assembly had been merely a motley crowd, a tessellated pavement without cement, a black stone here and a white stone there in which each member or each group was a law unto itself. There would have been nothing but chaos. This possibility of chaos was reduced to nil by the existence of the Congress Party inside the Assembly, which brought into its proceedings a sense of order and discipline. It is because of the discipline of the Congress Party that the Drafting Committee was able to pilot the Constitution in the Assembly with the sure knowledge as to the fate of each article and each amendment. The Congress Party is, therefore, entitled to all the credit for the smooth sailing of the Draft Constitution in the Assembly.

"On 26 January 1950, India will be an independent country. What would happen to her independence? Will she maintain her independence or will she lose it again? This is the first thought that comes to my mind. It is not that India was never an independent country. The point is that she once lost the independence she had. Will she lose it a second time? It is this thought which makes me most anxious for the future. What perturbs me greatly is the fact that not only India has once before lost her independence, but she lost it by the infidelity and treachery of some of her own people. In the invasion of Sind by Mahammed-Bin-Kasim, the military commanders of King Dahar accepted bribes from the agents of Mahommed-Bin-Kasim and refused to fight on the side of their King. It was Jaichand who invited Mahommed Ghori to invade India and fight against Prithvi Raj, and promised him the help of himself and the Solanki Kings. When Shivaji was fighting for the liberation of Hindus, the other Maratha noblemen and the Rajput Kings were fighting the battle on the side of Mughal Emperors. When the British were trying to destroy the Sikh rulers, Gulab Singh, their principal commander, sat silent and did not help to save the Sikh kingdom. In 1857, when a large part of India had declared a war of independence against the British, the Sikhs stood and watched the event as silent spectators.

"Will history repeat itself? It is this thought which fills me with anxiety. This anxiety is deepened by the realization of the fact that in addition to our old enemies in the form of castes and creeds we are going to have many political parties with diverse and opposing political creeds. Will Indians place the country above their creed or will they place creed above country? I do not know. But this much is certain that if the parties place creed above country, our independence will be put in jeopardy a second time and probably be lost forever. This eventuality we must all resolutely guard against. We must be determined to defend our independence with the last drop of our blood."

Ambedkar added: "On the 26th of January 1950, India would be a democratic country in the sense that India from that day would have a government of the people, by the people and for the people. The same thought comes to my mind. What would happen to her democratic constitution? Will she be able to maintain it or will she lose it again? This is the second thought that comes to my mind and makes me as anxious as the first.

"It is not that India did not know what democracy is. There was a time when India was studded with republics, and even where there were monarchies, they were either elected or limited. They were never absolute. It is not that India did not know parliament's parliamentary procedure. A study of the Buddhist Bhikkhu Sanghas discloses that not only there were parliaments for the Sanghas were nothing but parliaments—but the Sanghas knew and observed all the rules of the parliamentary procedure known to modern times. They had rules regarding seating arrangements, rules regarding motions, resolutions, quorum, whip, counting of votes, voting by ballot, censure motion, regularization, *res judicata,* etc. Although these rules of parliamentary procedure were applied by Buddha to the meetings of the Sanghas, he must have borrowed them from the rules of the political assemblies functioning in the country in his time.

"The democratic system India lost. Will she lose it a second time? I do not know. But it is quite possible in a country like India where democracy from its long disuse must be regarded, as something quite new-there is danger of democracy giving place to dictatorship. It is quite possible for this newborn democracy to return its form but give place to dictatorship in fact. If there is a landslide, the danger of the second possibility becoming actuality is much greater.

" If we wish to maintain democracy not merely in form, but also in fact, what must we do? The first thing in my judgement we must do is to hold fast to Constitutional methods of achieving our social and economical objectives. It means we must abandon the bloody methods of revolution.

It means we must abandon the methods of civil disobedience, non-cooperation and satyagraha. When there was no way left for Constitutional methods for achieving social and economic objectives, there was a great deal of justification for unconstitutional methods. But where Constitutional methods are open, there can be no justification for these unconstitutional methods. These methods are nothing but the Grammar of Anarchy and the sooner they are abandoned, the better for us.

"The second thing we must do is to observe the caution which John Stuart Mill has given to all who are interested in the maintenance of democracy, namely, not to lay their liberties at the feet of even a great man, or to trust him with powers which enable him to subvert their institutions. There is nothing wrong in being grateful to great men who have rendered life-long services to the country. But there are limits to gratefulness. As has been well said by the Irish patriot Daniel O'Connell, no man can be grateful at the cost of his honour, no woman can be grateful at the cost of her chastity and no nation can be grateful at the cost of its liberty. This caution is far more necessary in the case of India than in the case of any other country. For, in India, Bhakti or what may be called the path of devotion or hero-worship, plays a part in its politics unequalled in magnitude by the part it plays in the politics of any other country in the world. Bhakti in religion may be a road to the salvation of the soul. But in politics, Bhakti or hero-worship is a sure road to degradation and to eventual dictatorship.

"The third thing we must do is not to be content with merely political democracy. We must make our political democracy a social democracy as well. Political democracy cannot last unless there lies at the base of it social democracy. What does social democracy mean? It means a way of life, which recognizes a liberty, equality and fraternity as the principles of life. These principles of liberty, equality and fraternity are not to be treated as separate items in a trinity. They form a union of trinity in the sense that to divorce one from the other is to defeat a very purpose of democracy. Liberty cannot be divorced from the equality; equality cannot be divorced from the liberty. Nor can liberty and equality be divorced from fraternity. Without equality, liberty would produce the supremacy of the few over the many. Equality without liberty would kill individual initiative. Without fraternity, liberty and equality could not become a natural source of things. It would require a constable to enforce them. "We must begin by acknowledging the fact that there is complete absence of two things in Indian society based on the principle of graded inequality, which means elevation for some and degradation for others. On the economic plane, we have a society, in which there are some who have immense wealth as against many who live in abject poverty. On the 26th of January 1950, we are going to enter into the life of contradictions. In politics we will be recognizing the principle of one-man one-vote and one-vote one-value. In our social and economic life, we shall, by reason of our social and economical structure, continue to deny the principle of one-man one-value. How long shall we continue to live this life of contradictions? How long shall we continue to deny equality in our social and economic life? If we continue to deny it for long, we will do so only by putting our political democracy in peril. We must remove this contradiction at the earliest possible moment or else those who suffer from inequality will blow up the structure of political democracy which this Assembly has so laboriously built up."

Ambedkar continued: "Political power in this country has too long been the monopoly of a few and the many are not only beasts of burden, but also the beasts of prey. This monopoly has not merely deprived them of their chance of betterment; it has sapped them of what may be called the significance of life. These downtrodden classes are tired of being governed. They are impatient to govern themselves. This urge for self-realization in the downtrodden classes must not be allowed to devolve into a class struggle or class war. It would lead to a division of the house. That would indeed be a day of disaster for us, as has been well said by Abraham Lincoln, a house divided against itself cannot stand very long. Therefore the sooner room is made for the realization of their aspiration, the better for few, the better for the country, the better for the maintenance of its independence and the better for the continuance of its democratic structure. This can only be done by the establishment of equality and fraternity in all spheres of life. This is why I have laid so much stress on them.

"Independence is no doubt a matter of joy. But let us not forget that this independence has thrown on us great responsibilities. By independence, we have lost the excuse of blaming the British for anything going wrong. If hereafter things go wrong, we will have nobody to blame except ourselves. There is great danger of things going wrong. Times are fast changing. People including our own are being moved by new ideologies. They are getting tired of government by the people. They are prepared to have government for the people and are indifferent whether it is a government of the people or by the people. If we wish to preserve the Constitution in which we have sought to enshrine the principle of government of the people, for the people, and by the people, let us resolve not to be tardy in the recognition of the evils that lie across our path and which induce people to prefer government for the people to government by the people, nor to be weak in our initiative to remove them. That is the only way to serve the country. I know of no better. (*Dr. Babasaheb Ambedkar: Writings & Speeches*, Vol. 13, pp. 1206-18)

These pregnant statements of Ambedkar are so significant and relevant that one cannot afford to overlook their implications to the very fabric of our democracy, Constitution and the quality—nay to the society as a whole. Unless we take a serious note of his warnings and act betimes, his prophetic words may become a reality, which if and when it happens would be a calamity.

Parliament

Qualifications for Membership of Parliament and State Legislatures

Speaking in Parliament on 23 November 1950, Ambedkar said: "It seems to me that education can hardly be the sole qualification for the membership of this House. According to Buddha man requires two things. One is *Gyan* and the other is *Sheel. Gyan* without *Sheel* is very dangerous. It must be accompanied by *Sheel*, by which we mean, character, moral courage, ability to be independent by any kind of temptation, truthful to one's ideals. But even though I am very keen to see that no member enters this August Assembly who does not possess *Sheel* in adequate degree, I find it extremely difficult to find any means or methods to ensure that valuable contribution."

Ambedkar added said: "I regard education to be a very necessary qualification for possessing that degree of competence which is very necessary for the performance of one's duty. In this House there are people who, although they are not educated are very competent to voice the grievances of the class whom they represent. A more educated person will not be able to discharge that function, because he does not know and does not have that experience. What is necessary for bringing relief to the call of people whom they represent is not merely making speeches in the House but to suggest remedies for the removal of grievances. To make speeches and to ventilate grievances is a very easy matter but to formulate remedies is very difficult matter. It requires education and therefore education even from the standpoint of the backward classes, scheduled classes or tribal classes is a very necessary ingredient."

In conclusion, he said: "My suggestion is that this is a matter which had better be left to the people themselves or to the political parties who will run the government. I have no doubt about it that if the political parties, for their own particular purposes, do not attend to this matter, people themselves in course of time will attend to it. People are not going to allow persons who cannot discharge their functions properly in this House to be continued and returned for ever.

They want results. They want their welfare to be attended to, and I am sure about it that they will realize that the only instrumentality through which they can achieve this purpose is to send good men to this House."

Again speaking in Parliament on 21 May 1952 after relinquishing his post as Law Minister, Ambedkar said: "No hungry man is going to be sympathetic to a critic who is going to tell him: 'My dear fellow, although I am in power, although I am in authority, although I possess all legal power to set matter right, you must not expect me to do a miracle because I have inherited a past which is very inglorious.'

If the government will not produce results within a certain time, long before the people become so frustrated, so disgusted with government as not to have any government at all, a time will come when I suppose unless we in parliament realize our responsibilities and shoulder the task of looking after the welfare and good of the people within a reasonable time, I have not the slightest doubt in my own mind that this parliament would be treated by the public outside with utter contempt. It would be a thing not wanted at all."

Ambedkar wanted black-marketers and holders of permits and licences to be disqualified from contesting elections along with contractors. But he was forced to remove the clause because of strong opposition from Congress members. Another battle which he fought bitterly but lost in the end was in regard to expenses incurred during elections by political parties.

Rajya Sabha

Ruling Nation and Subject Nation

Speaking on the third report of the Commissioner for Scheduled Castes and Tribes in Rajya Sabha on 6 September 1954, Ambedkar said: "Here in this country you find really two nations-a ruling nation and a nation which is a subject nation. The backward classes are all subject people. They have no authority in any place. None whatsoever. They have no place in administration. They have no place in the Executive and the Executive and Administration is entirely monopolized by the higher classes. They are monopolizing it be reason of the fact that they have been able to get the highest education. Why not examine all the secretaries of the departments in the government of India? The son and daughter of every secretary in the government is to be found in Cambridge or Oxford. Twice or thrice they have made journeys in order to lodge their children there because they have the amplest means. The backward class man's son cannot get even primary education. This sort of revolution in the two different classes is going on for centuries—it is an intolerable business because we cannot allow one class to rule forever. For some time they may but they must see that the other classes also become educationally qualified in order that they too may hold the reins of government. We are not going to be subject people for all the time."

What Ambedkar said in 1954 has been in prevalent all these years. The only difference is that the children of the Secretaries and High officials have now preference for going to America.

Speaking on the same day in parliament on the Indian Administrative Service (IAS) and Indian Police Service (IPS) Ambedkar said: "Has there been any recruitment to the IAS since 1952? I have not seen a single scheduled caste candidate being chosen by the Public Service Commission for the IAS—not one. I have not seen a single candidate being chosen by the Public Service Commission for the IPS either. It is only last year that I struggled with Public Service Commission and induced them to accept one for the IPS."

Elaborating the difference between the Executive Service and the Administrative Service, Ambedkar said: "There is difference between the executive service and the administrative service. An administrative service is more or less a clerical thing. The executive service possesses the power of direction. It has directive authority. Two thousand clerks are of no value as compared to one officer holding an executive post. In Hindi we call it *Maarneki Jagah*. What are these poor clerks? You will see in fortresses—but you have none in UP—in my part of the country the place is full of Maratha fortresses."

Ambedkar added: "These executive posts are posts from where direction can be given. The clerks need all kinds of protection. Any officer may spoil their character-roll by writing a bad remark or saying that the man is no good. The only way he can be protected is by having somebody in the executive service who might look into this matter and see no injustice is being done. If the executive authority is unsympathetic, is antagonistic, that policy, however good it may be, can never fructify. The whole of the administration which is composed of caste Hindus, is the most unsympathetic administration that the scheduled castes have to suffer under. Until and unless the executive becomes more sympathetic to the scheduled castes, none of the laws and none of the administrative policies will bear any fruit."

Economic Emancipation

Speaking in parliament on the third report of the Commissioner of Scheduled Castes and Tribes Ambedkar said: "Economic emancipation of scheduled castes will depend upon the opportunity they get for what might be called entry into gainful occupation. Unless and until the doors are open to them where they can find gainful occupation, their economic emancipation is not going to take place. They are going to remain slaves, if not slaves, serfs of the landowning classes in the villages. Out of these gainful occupations, most important is the giving of land to the scheduled castes. They must be settled on the land so that they might obtain independent means of livelihood, cease to be afraid of anybody, walk with their heads erect and live fearlessly and courageously. Government by law should limit the holding of those who hold land and take away the excess and hand it over to the scheduled castes. Secondly, the government may finance the purchase of land if any is to be sold."

Ambedkar added: "The land holding in India is not merely a matter of economic livelihood. It is a matter of social status. A person holding land has a higher status than a person not holding land. In the villages the matter of economic status is of the utmost importance to everybody. And no Hindu wishes that an untouchable should possess a piece of land so that he may reach a higher status than his community is entitled to under the social system. The government has committed one of the greatest acts of folly in creating the peasants proprietors, just to win political elections."

Ambedkar also said: "The peasant proprietorship in this country is going to bring about complete ruination of the country. What we want is—although I am not a communist—the Russian system of collective farming. That is the only way by which we can solve our agricultural problem."

Ambedkar suggested to the government: "Unless you want to go on fooling the scheduled castes by telling them, 'Oh, keep quiet, we are going to give you a piece of land. Either we will have ceiling or we will finance your purchase. We will do this or do that unless you want to go on fooling them this, you ought to think of some other method of doing that. This is a problem you must solve and if you do not solve it, you know what consequences there might be—most evil consequences. The fire is burning outside; it may easily come in and the scheduled castes may carry the banner and you and your Constitution will go under. Nothing will remain.' "

Gandhi Trust Fund

Ambedkar said in parliament on 6 September 1954: "The abolition of salt tax was done in the memory of Mr. Gandhi. I respect him and suggest to you that you levy the tax and create a Trust Fund in the name of Mr. Gandhi—'Gandhi Trust Fund'—for the development or settlement of the untouchables. After all, the untouchables, were the nearest and dearest to him and there is no reason why Mr. Gandhi may not bless this project from heaven, namely, levying the tax and using it for the development of waste land and settling the scheduled castes on this waste land. This will perpetuate the name of Gandhi and will give relief to the people whom he wanted to protect and whom he wanted to elevate."

Need for Second Capital

Making out a case for the second capital Dr. Ambedkar said: "Since the departure of the British, India has only one capital and that is Delhi. Before the British, India has always had two capitals. During the Mughal period, India had Delhi as one capital and Srinagar in Kashmir as another capital. When the British came they too had two capitals. One was Calcutta and another was Simla. Even when they left Calcutta for Delhi, they retained Simla as their summer capital. The two capitals maintained by the Mughals and British were the results of climatic conditions. Neither the British nor the Mughals were able to live in Delhi or in Calcutta, continuously for two months. The summer months in Delhi were unbearable to the Mughals. They made Srinagar their second capital for summer months. The summer months in Calcutta were equally unbearable to the British. They, therefore, established second capital. To these climatic conditions must now be added three other conditions. There was no popular government when the Mughals ruled or the British ruled. Now we have popular government and the convenience of the people is an important factor. Delhi is most inconvenient to the people of South. They suffer the most from cold as well as distance. Even the Northern people suffer in the summer months. They do not complain because they are nearer home and they are nearer the seat of power. Second is feeling of the southern people and third is the consideration of defence. The feeling of the southern people is that the capital of their country is far away from them and they are being ruled by people of northern India.

The third consideration is of course more important. It is that Delhi is a vulnerable place. It is within bombing distance of the neighboring countries. Although India is trying to live in peace with its neighbours. It cannot be assumed that India will not to have face war some time or the other and if war comes, the government of India will have to leave Delhi and find other place for its location. Which is the place to which the government of India can migrate? A place that one can think of is Calcutta. But Calcutta is also within bombing distance from Tibet.

"Although India and China today are friends how long the friendship would last no one can definitely say. The possibility of conflict between India and China remains. In that event Calcutta would be useless. The next town that could be considered as refuge for the central government is Bombay. But Bombay is a port and our Indian Navy is too poor to protect the central government if it came down to Bombay. Is there a fourth place one could think of? I find Hyderabad to be such a place. Hyderabad, Secunderabad and Bolaram should be constituted into a Chief Commissioner Province and made a second capital of India. Hyderabad fulfils all the requirement of a capital for India. Hyderabad is equidistant to all states.

"From the defence point of view it would give safety to the central government. It is equidistant from all parts of India.

It would give the satisfaction to the South Indian people that their government is sometimes with them. The government may remain in Delhi during winter months and during other months it can stay in Hyderabad. Hyderabad has all the amenities, which Delhi has and it is a far better city than Delhi. It has all the grandeur which Delhi has. Buildings are going cheap and they are really beautiful buildings, far superior to those in Delhi.

"Hyderabad, Secunderabad and Bolaram should be constituted into a second capital of India. Fortunately, it can be very easily done with the satisfaction to the whole of South India, to Maharashtra and to Andhra." (*Dr. Babasaheb Ambedkar: Writings & Speeches,* Vol. 1, pp. 170-71)

Partition of India

Dr. Ambedkar was happy on the partition of India. He expressed his happiness in the following words: "I was glad that India was separated from Pakistan. I was the philosopher so to say, of Pakistan. I advocated partition, because I felt that it was only by partition that Hindus would not only be independent but free. If India and Pakistan had remained united in one state Hindus though independent would have been at the mercy of the Muslims. A merely independent India would not have been a free India from the point of view of the Hindus. It would have been a government of one country by two nations and of these two the Muslims without the question would have been the ruling race notwithstanding Hindu Mahasabha and Jana Sangh. When the partition took place I felt that God was willing to lift his curse and let India be one, great and prosperous. But I fear that the curse may fall again. For I find that those who are advocating linguistic states have at heart the ideal of making the regional language as their official language.

"This will be death knell to the idea of United India. With regional languages as official languages the ideal to make India one united country and to make Indians, Indians first and Indians last, will vanish." (*Dr. Babasaheb Ambedkar: Writings & Speeches*, Vol. 1, pp 146)

Drawing attention to the concept of 'Nation' Dr. Ambedkar said: "...I remember the days when politically minded Indians resented the expression 'the people of India'. They preferred the expression 'the Indian nation.' I am of opinion that in believing that we are a nation, we are cherishing a great delusion. How can people divided into several thousands of castes be a nation? The sooner we realize that we are not as yet a nation in the social and psychological sense of the word, the better for us. For then only we shall realize the necessity of becoming a nation and seriously think of ways and means of realizing the goal. The realization of this goal is going to be very difficult—far more difficult than it has been in the United States. The United States has no caste problem. In India there are castes. These castes are anti-national: in the first place because they bring about the separation in social life. They are anti-national because they generate jealousy and antipathy between caste and caste. But we must overcome all these difficulties if we wish to become a nation in reality. For fraternity, equality and liberty will be no deeper than coats of paints. "

It is sad that during over six decades of independence, instead of freeing the minds of people in general and youths in particular from the fetters of casteism, the feelings of casteism have been strengthened for administrative and political gains. No less a person than Dr. S. Radhakrishnan a distinguished philosopher pointed out when he was President of India, "Caste has ceased to be a social evil, but has become a political and administrative evil. We want to get votes and we set up candidates suited to the people who have to vote.... It is essential that politics should be as far as possible lifted out of this kind of morass."

It may be recollected what Dr. Ambedkar had said in Bombay Legislative Assembly on 6 October 1932: "...If India has not succeeded in producing nationalism, if India has not succeeded in building up a national spirit, the chief reason for that is the existence of the village system. It made all people saturated with local particularism, with local patriotism. It left no room for larger civic spirit. None whatever. Under the ancient village panchayats, India, instead of being a country of united people, became a loose conglomeration of village communities with no common tie except common allegiance to a common king.

"... In these days when you are striving for bringing about national spirit, in these days when you are striving for bringing about a common nationality and common sense of Indian citizenship, we ought to do nothing which will nullify and which will dilute that sense." (*Dr. Babasaheb Ambedkar: Writings & Speeches,* Vol. 1, p. 106)

Dr. Ambedkar insisted, if the village panchayat came into existence, there should be a special representation for the minorities. At any rate there should special representation for the depressed classes. Dr. Ambedkar said, "There is a section in this House who will at once jump and say that this is communalism. I agree that this is communalism. But I am also convinced that communalism must be my policy. I am not ashamed of it. I will say that India can not proceed on the path of political progress without communalism. Without communalism there can be no self-government for India. That is the position I would assert without fear of challenge." (*Dr. Babasaheb Ambedkar: Writings & Speeches*, Vol. 1, pp. 106-07)

Dr. Ambedkar's Views on Amendment of the Constitution

During the tenure of Dr. Ambedkar as Law Minister and a member of parliament, four Bills were moved for amendment of the Constitution.

Constitution (First Amendment) Bill 1951

The First Amendment was necessitated because of certain judgment of the Supreme Court. Speaking in the parliament, Dr. Ambedkar said: "...I have carefully studied both these judgments of the Supreme Court and with all respect to the judges of the Supreme Court I cannot help saying that I find this judgment to be utterly unsatisfactory... . The judgment does not appear to be in consonance with the articles of the Constitution..." This was before Dr. Ambedkar tendered his resignation as Law Minister.

Speaking on the Bill he said: "....Now I come to the manner in which the government has been proceeding with the amendment of the Constitution. The Constitution is only about four years—not an adult yet, and in the four years and seven months of its life this is the third amendment of the Constitution. I do not know any Constitution in the world which has been amended so rapidly and, if I may say so, so rashly, by the Government in office."

He added, "Is our government observing these fundamental rules? It is quite true that our Constitution is a very fluid one. It is not half as the American Constitution or the Australian Constitution, and those who were in charge of framing the Constitution were fully conscious of the fact that circumstances would arise which would require amendment of the Constitution, and you cannot allow the Constitution to hold up the solution of social problems which are emergent. It was because of that it was proposed that the provisions contained in Article 368 should suffice... But I have not the least doubt in my mind that no one who had anything to do with the Drafting of the Constitution ever thought that the government would rush in on the spur of the moment to amend the Constitution without giving notice to the voters. Notice to voters, if I may submit, is a general principle of political life and party life. Every party must have a mandate to do a certain thing. You cannot take the voters by surprise and you cannot assume absolute authority to amend even the Constitution simply because you are elected. This exactly what our government has been doing. Simply because they have obtained a majority they assume that they have not only the power to make any law whatsoever relating to any of the entries which gave them the power to make laws but they have also got the power, merely by being elected, even without notifying their intention to the people as much, to even amend the Constitution. Is the Constitution not different in any sense from any ordinary law? Is it merely a scrap of paper to be amended at the whim of anybody? There is a saying in Marathi....we say, if the old woman dies it really does not matter very much but what we are afraid is that Yama gets habituated to coming often and often and what we want to prevent is the Yama's invasion. It does not matter if the old woman is dead or snatched away. This is exactly what has been happening and I have been noticing the great contempt or the low regard or respect which the government has for the Constitution".

Constitution (Fourth Amendment) Bill 1954

Speaking on the Constitution (Fourth Amendment) Bill, Dr. Ambedkar said: "I do not suppose the government has cared to pay any heed. I would like to repeat the same caution again and I should like to give some reasons why the Constitution should not be amended and tampered so easily... That is the reason why I say that the Constitution should not be so lightly and so frequently amended. I do not know whether the Government would listen to it, perhaps not".

He added, "In other countries wherever a clause of the Constitution has been interpreted by the judiciary in a way which the government does not like, the government concurs in, it does not like to upset the decision of the court. Here, in our country, we have cultivated a different mentality. Our mentality is that if the judges of the Supreme Court do not give a judgment, which is to our liking, then we can throw it out. That is what it is. I am rather glad with regard to the behavior of our Supreme Court. In the short time that it has been in the existence, I see some different phases of the Supreme Court.... I remember that in the very first flush of its power, the Supreme Court declared or had the courage to declare that a certain section of the Indian Penal Code was *ultra virus.* Our government at once reacted and brought in an Amendment to declare that the interpretation of the Supreme Court was wrong. I hope notwithstanding the constant amendments which the government seems to be prone to bringing forth, the Supreme Court will continue to have its independent judgment, notwithstanding what the government may have to say. I do not find that the Supreme Court has given any judgment which, any independent man can say, is not in consonance with the terms of the Constitution."

In his speech on 'landholding,' "The government is going to amend the Constitution. They are fond of amending the Constitution. Why have a Constitution at all, if you are amending it every Saturday."

With regard to the intellectuals Dr. Ambedkar said "In every country, the intellectual class is the most influential class, if not the governing class. The intellectual class is the class which can foresee, it is the class, which can advice and give lead. In no country does the mass of the people live the life of intelligent thought and action. It is largely imitative and follows the intellectual class. There is no exaggeration in saying that the entire destiny of a country depends upon its intellectual class. If the intellectual class is honest, independent and disinterested, it can be trusted to take the initiative and give a proper lead when a crisis arises. It is true that intellect by itself is no virtue. It is only a means and the use of means depends upon the ends, which an intellectual person pursues. An intellectual man can be a good man but he can easily be a rogue. Similarly, an intellectual class may be a band of high-souled persons, ready to help, ready to emancipate erring humanity or it may easily be a gang of crooks or a body of advocates of a narrow clique from which it draws its support." (*Dr. Babasaheb Ambedkar: Writings & Speeches*, Vol. 1, p. 71)

The country is passing through difficult times. I have confidence that intellectuals with faith, vision and courage will rise to restore order and lead the country to the glory, which is hers by right.

Annexure I

Ambedkar's Statement on Resignation

The House I am sure knows, unofficially if not officially, that I have ceased to be a Member of the Cabinet. I tendered my resignation on Thursday the 27th of September to the Prime Minister and asked him to relieve me immediately. The Prime Minister was good enough to accept the same on the very next day. If I have continued to be a Minister after Friday the 28th, it is because the Prime Minister had requested me to continue till the end of the Session—a request to which I was, in obedience to constitutional convention, bound to assent.

Our Rules of Procedure permit a Minister who has resigned his office, to make a personal statement in explanation of his resignation. Many members of Cabinet have resigned during my tenure of office. There have been, however, no uniform practice in the matter of Ministers who have resigned making a statement. For a few days I was hesitant what course to follow. After taking all circumstances into consideration I came to the conclusion that the making of a statement was not merely necessary, but it was a duty which a member who has resigned owes to the House.

The House has no opportunity to know how the Cabinet works from within, whether there is harmony or whether there is a conflict, for the simple reason that there is a joint responsibility under which a member who is in a minority is not entitled to disclose his differences. Consequently, the House continues to think that there is no conflict among the members of Cabinet even when as a matter of fact a conflict exists. It is, therefore, a duty of a retiring Minister to make a statement informing the House why he wants to go and why he is not able to continue to take further joint responsibility.

Secondly, if a Minister goes without making a statement, people may suspect that there is something wrong with the conduct of the Minister, either in his public capacity or in his private capacity. No Minister should, I think, leave room for such suspicion and the only safe way out is a statement.

Thirdly, we have our newspapers. They have their age-old bias in favour of some and against others. Their judgments are seldom based on merits. Wherever they find an empty space, they are prone to fill the vacuum by supplying grounds but which put those whom they favour in a better light and those not in their favour in a bad light. Some such thing I see has happened even in my case.

It is for these reasons that I decided to make a statement before going out.

It is now 4 years, 1 month and 26 days since I was called by the Prime Minister to accept the office of Law Minister in his Cabinet. The offer came as a great surprise to me. I was in the opposite camp and had already been condemned as unworthy of association when the interim Government was formed in August 1946. I was left to speculate as to what could have happened to bring about this change in the attitude of the Prime Minister. I had my doubts. I did not know how I could carry on with those who had never been my friends. I had doubts as to whether I could, as a Law Member, maintain the standard of legal knowledge and acumen which had been maintained by those who had preceded me as Law Ministers of the Government of India. But I kept my doubts at rest and accepted the offer of the Prime Minister on the ground that I should not deny my cooperation when it was asked for in the building up our nation. The quality of my performance as a Member of the Cabinet and as Law Minister, I must leave it to others to judge.

I will not refer to matters which have led me to sever my connection with my colleagues. The urge to go has been growing from long past due to variety of reasons.

I will first refer to matters purely of a personal character and which are the least of the grounds which have led me to tender my resignation. As a result of my being a member of Viceroy's Council, I knew the Law Ministry to be administratively of no importance. It gave no opportunity for shaping the policy of the Government of India. We used to call it an empty soap box only good for old lawyers to play with. When the Prime Minister made me the offer, I told him that besides being a lawyer by my education and experience, I was competent to run any administrative Department and that in the old Viceroy's Executive Council I held two administrative portfolios, that of Labour and C.P.W.D., where a great deal of planning projects were dealt with by me and would like to have some administrative portfolio. The Prime Minister agreed and said he would give me in addition to Law the Planning Department which, he said, he was intending to create. Unfortunately the Planning Department came very late in the day and when it did come I was left out. During my time, there have been many transfers of portfolios from one Minister to another. I thought I might be considered for any one of them. But I have always been left out of consideration. Many ministers have been given two or three portfolios so that they have been overburdened. Others like me have been wanting more work. I have not even been considered for holding a portfolio temporarily when a Minister in charge has gone abroad for a few days. It is difficult to understand what the principle is underlying the distribution of Government work among Ministers which the Prime Minister follows. Is it capacity? Is it trust? Is it friendship? Is it pliability? I was not even appointed to be a member of main Committees of the Cabinet such as the Foreign Affairs Committee or the Defense Committee. When the Economic Affairs Committee was formed, I expected, in view of the fact that I was primarily a student of Economics and Finance, to be appointed to this Committee. But I was left out. I was appointed to it by the Cabinet, when the Prime Minister had gone to England. But when he returned, in one of his many essays in the reconstruction of the Cabinet, he left me out. In a subsequent reconstruction my name was added to Committee, but that was as a result of my protest.

The Prime Minister, I am sure, will agree that I have never complained to him in this connection. I have never been a party to the game of power politics inside the Cabinet or the game of snatching portfolios which goes on when there is a vacancy. I believe in service, service in the post which the Prime Minister, who as the head of the Cabinet, thought fit to assign to me. It would have, however, been quite inhuman for me not to have felt that a wrong was being done to me.

I will now refer to another matter that had made me dissatisfied with the Government. It relates to the treatment accorded to the Backward Classes and the Scheduled Castes. I was very sorry that the Constitution did not embody any safeguards for the Backward Classes. It was left to be done by the Executive Government on the basis of the recommendations of a Commission to be appointed by the President. More than a year has elapsed since we passed the Constitution. But the Government has not yet even thought of appointing the Commission. The year 1946 during which I was out of office, was a year of great anxiety to me and to the leading members of the Scheduled Castes. The British had resiled from the commitments they had made in the matter of constitutional safeguards for the Scheduled Castes and the Scheduled Castes had no knowing as to what the Constituent Assembly would do in that behalf. In this period of anxiety I had prepared a report on the condition of the Scheduled Castes for submission to the United Nations. But I did not submit it. I felt that it would be better to wait until the Constituent Assembly and the future Parliament was given a chance to deal with the matter. The provisions made in the Constitution for safeguarding the position of the Scheduled Castes were not to my satisfaction. However, I accepted them for what they were worth, hoping that the Government will show some determination to make them effective. What is the position of the Scheduled Castes today? So far as I see, it is the same as before. The same old tyranny, the same oppression, the same old discrimination which existed before, exists now, and perhaps in a worst form. I can refer to hundreds of cases where people from the Scheduled Castes round about Delhi and adjoining places have come to me with their tales of woes against the Caste Hindus and against the Police who have refused to register their complaints and render them any help. I have been wondering whether there is any other parallel in the world to the conditions of the Scheduled Castes in India. I cannot find any. And yet why is no relief granted to the Scheduled Castes? Compare the concern the Government shows over safeguarding the Muslims. The Prime Minister's whole time and attention is devoted for the protection of the Muslims. I yield to none, not even to the Prime Minister, in my desire to give the Muslims of India the utmost protection wherever and whenever they stand in need of it. But what I want to know is, are Muslims the only people who need protection? Are the Scheduled Castes, the Scheduled Tribes and the Indian Christians not in need of protection? What concern has he shown for these communities? So far as I know, none and yet these are the communities which need far more care and attention than the Muslims.

I could not contain within myself the indignation I have felt over the neglect of the Scheduled Castes by the Government and on one occasion I gave vent to my feelings at a public meeting of the Scheduled Castes. A question was asked, from the Hon'ble the Home Minister, whether my charge that the Scheduled Castes had not benefitted by the rule which guaranteed to them 12 1/2 per cent representation was true. In answer to the question the Hon'ble the Home Minister was pleased to say that my charge was baseless. Subsequently for some reason- it may be for satisfying the qualms of his conscience- he, I am informed, sent round a circular to the various Departments of the Government of India asking them to report how many Scheduled Castes candidates had been recently recruited in Government service. I am informed that most Departments said in reply 'NIL' or nearly nil. If the information is correct, I need make no commentary on the answer given by the Hon'ble the Home Minister.

From my early childhood I have dedicated myself to the upliftment of the Scheduled Castes among whom I was born. It is not that there were no temptations in my way. If I had considered my own interest, I could have been anything I wanted to be and if I had joined the Congress, I would have reached to the highest place in that organization. But as I said, I had dedicated myself to the upliftment of the scheduled castes and I have followed the adage which says that it is better to be narrow-minded if you wish to be enthusiastic about the cause which you wish to accomplish. You can, therefore, well imagine what pain it has caused me to see that the cause of the scheduled castes has been relegated to the limbo of nothing.

The third matter which has given me cause, not merely for dissatisfaction but for actual anxiety and even worry, is the foreign policy of the country. Any one, who has followed the course of our foreign policy and along with it the attitude of other countries towards India, could not fail to realize the sudden change that has taken place in their attitude towards us. On 15th of August 1947 when we began our life as an independent country, there was no country which wished us ill. Every country in the world was our friend. Today, after four years, all our friends have deserted us. We have no friends left. We have alienated ourselves. We are pursuing a lonely furrow with no one even to second our resolutions in the UNO. When I think of our foreign policy, I am reminded of what Bismark and Bernard Shaw have said. Bismark has said that "politics is not a game of realizing the ideal. Politics is the game of the possible." Bernard Shaw not very long ago said that good ideals are good but one must not forget that it is often dangerous to be too good. Our foreign policy is in complete opposition to the words of wisdom uttered by two of the world's greatest men.

How dangerous it has done to us by this policy of doing the impossible and of being too good is illustrated by the great drain on our resources made by our military expenditure, by the difficulty of getting food for our starving millions and by difficulty of getting aid for the industrialization of our country.

Out of 350 crores of rupees of revenue we raise annually, we spend about Rs. 180 crores of rupees on the Army. It is colossal expenditure which has hardly any parallel. This colossal expenditure is the direct result of our foreign policy. We have to foot the whole of our Bill for our defence ourselves because we have no friends on which we can depend for help in any emergency that may arise. I have been wondering whether this is the right sort of foreign policy.

Our quarrel with Pakistan is a part of our foreign policy about which I feel deeply dissatisfied. There are two grounds which have disturbed our relations with Pakistan—one is Kashmir and the other is the condition of our people in East Bengal. I felt that we should be more deeply concerned with East Bengal where the condition of our people seems from all the newspaper reports intolerable than with Kashmir. Notwithstanding this we have been staking our all on the Kashmir Issue. Even then I feel that we have been fighting on an unreal issue. This issue on which we are fighting most of the time is, who is the right and who is the wrong. The real issue to my mind is not who is the right but what is right. Taking that to be the main question my view has always been that the right solution is to partition Kashmir. Give the Hindu and Buddhist part to India and the Muslim part to Pakistan as we did in the case of India. We are really not concerned with the Muslim part of Kashmir. It is the matter between the Muslims of Kashmir and Pakistan. They may decide the issue as they like. Or if you like, divide it into three parts; the Cease-fire zone, the valley and the Jammu-Ladhak Region and have a plebiscite only in the vally. What I am afraid of is that in the proposed plebiscite, which is to be an overall plebiscite, the Hindus and Buddhists of Kashmir are likely to be dragged into Pakistan against their wishes and we may have to face the same problems as we are facing today in East Bengal.

I will now refer to the Fourth matter which has a good deal to do with my resignation. The Cabinet has become a merely recording and registration office of decisions already arrived at by Committees. As I have said, the Cabinet now works by Committees. There is a Defence Committee. There is a Foreign Committee. All important matters relating to Foreign affairs are dealt with by it. All matters relating to

Defence are disposed of by the Defence Committee. The same members of the Cabinet are appointed by them. I am not a member of either of these Committees. They work behind an iron curtain. Others who are not members have only to take joint responsibility without any opportunity of taking part in the shaping of policy. This is an impossible position.

I will now deal with a matter which has led me finally to come to the decision that I should resign. It is the treatment which was accorded to the Hindu Code. The Bill was introduced in this House on the 11th of April 1947. After a life of four years, it was killed and died unwept and unsung, after 4 clauses of it were passed. While it was before the House, it lived by fits and starts. For one full year the Government did not feel it necessary to refer it to a Select Committee. It was referred to the Select Committee on the 9th of April 1948. The Report was presented to the House on 12th of August 1948. The motion for the consideration of the Report was made by me on 31st of August 1948. It was merely for making the motion that the Bill was kept on the Agenda. The discussion of the motion was not allowed to take place until the February Session of the year 1949. Even then it was not allowed to have a continuous discussion. It was distributed over 10 months, 4 days in February, 1 day in March and 2 days in April 1949. After this, one day was given to the Bill in December 1949, namely, the 19th of December on which the House adopted my motion that the Bill as reported by the Select Committee be taken into consideration. No time was given to the Bill in the year 1950. Next time the Bill came before the House was on the 5th of February 1951 when the clause by clause consideration of the Bill was taken. Only three days 5th, 6th and 7th of February were given to the Bill and left there to rot.

This being the last Session of the Parliament, Cabinet had to consider whether the Hindu Code Bill should be got through before this Parliament ended or whether it should be left over to the new Parliament. The Cabinet unanimously decided that it should be put through in this Parliament. So the Bill was put on the Agenda and was taken up on the 17th of September 1951 for further clause by clause consideration. As the discussion was going on the Prime Minister put forth a new proposal, namely, that the Bill as a whole may not be got through within the time available and that it was desirable to get a part of it enacted into law rather than the whole of it to go to waste. It was a great wrentch to me. But I agreed, for, as the proverb says: "It is better to save a part when the whole is likely to be lost."

The Prime Minister suggested that we should select the Marriage and Divorce part. The Bill in its truncated form went on. After two or three days of discussion of the Bill the Prime Minister came up with another proposal. This time his proposal was to drop the whole Bill even the Marriage and Divorce portion. This came to me as a great shock—a bolt from the blue. I was stunned and could not say anything. I am not prepared to accept that the dropping of this truncated Bill was due to want of time. I am sure that the truncated Bill was dropped because other and more powerful members of the Cabinet wanted precedence for their Bills. I am unable to understand how the Benares and Aligarh University Bills, how the Press Bill could have been given precedence over the

Hindu Code even in its attenuated form? It is not that there was no law on the Statute Book to govern the Aligarh University or the Benares University. It is not that these universities would have gone to wreck and ruins if the Bills had not been passed in this Session. It is not that the Press Bill was urgent. There is already a law on the Statute Book and the Bill could have waited. I got the impression that the Prime Minister, although sincere, had not the earnestness and the determination required to get the Hindu Code Bill through.

In regard to this Bill I have been made to go through the greatest mental torture. The aid of Party machinery was denied to me. The Prime Minister gave freedom of vote, an unusual thing in the history of the Party. I did not mind it. But I expected two things. I expected a party whip as to time limit on speeches and instruction to the Chief Whip to move closure when sufficient debate had taken place. A whip on time limit on speeches would have got the Bill through. When freedom of voting was given there could have been no objection to have given a whip for time limit on speeches. But such a whip was never issued. The conduct of the Minister for Parliamentary Affairs, who is also the Chief Whip of the Party in connection with the Hindu Code, to say the least, has been most extraordinary. He has been the deadliest opponent of the Code and has never been present to aid me by moving a closure motion. For days and hours filibustering has gone on a single clause. But the Chief Whip, whose duty it is to economise Government time and push on Government Business, has been systematically absent when the Hindu Code has been under consideration in the House. I have never seen a case of a Chief Whip so disloyal to the Prime Minister and a Prime

Minister so loyal to a disloyal whip. Notwithstanding this unconstitutional behaviour, the Chief Whip is really a darling of the Prime Minister. For notwithstanding his disloyalty he got a promotion in the Party organization. It is impossible to carry on in such circumstances.

It has been said that the Bill had to be dropped because the opposition was strong. How strong was the opposition? This Bill has been discussed several times in the Party and was carried to division by the opponents. Every time the opponents were routed. The last time when the Bill was taken up in the Party meeting, out of 120 only 20 were found to be against it. When the Bill was taken in the Party for discussion, 44 clauses were passed in about three and half hours time. This shows how much opposition there was to the Bill within the Party. In the House itself there have been divisions on three clauses of the Bill—2, 3 and 4. Every time there has been a overwhelming majority in favour even on clause 4 which is the soul of Hindu Code.

I was therefore, quite unable to accept the Prime Minister's decision to abandon the Bill on the ground of time. I have been obliged to give this elaborate explanation for my resignation because some people have suggested that I am going because of my illness. I wish to repudiate any such suggestion. I am the last man to abandon my duty because of illness.

It may be said that my resignation is out of time and that if I was dissatisfied with Foreign Policy of the Government and the treatment accorded to the Backward Classes and the Scheduled Castes I should have gone earlier. The charge may sound as true. But I had reasons which held me back. In the first place, most of the time I have been a member of the Cabinet, I have been busy with the framing of the Constitution. It absorbed all my attention till 26th of January 1950 and thereafter I was concerned with the People's Representation Bill and the Delimitation Orders. I had hardly any time to attend to our Foreign Affairs. I did not think it right to go away leaving this work unfinished.

In the second place, I thought it necessary to stay on, for the sake of the Hindu Code. In the opinion of some it may be wrong for me to have held on for the sake of the Hindu Code. I took a different view. The Hindu Code was a greatest social reform measure ever undertaken by the Legislature in this country. No law passed by the Indian Legislature in the past or likely to be passed in the future can be compared to it in point of its significance. To leave inequality between class and class, between sex and sex which, is the soul of Hindu Society untouched and to go on passing legislation relating to economic problems is to make a farce of our Constitution and to build a palace on a dung heap. This is the significance I attach to the Hindu Code. It is for its sake that I stayed on notwithstanding my differences. So if I have committed a wrong it is in the hope of doing some good. Had I no ground for such a hope, for overcoming the obstructionist tactics of the opponents? I would like in this connection to refer only to three of the statements made by the Prime Minister on the floor of this House.

On 28th November, 1949 the Prime Minister gave the following assurance. He said: "What is more, the Government is committed to this thing (Hindu Code). It is going through with it. "Government would proceed with that. It is for the House to accept a measure, but if a Government takes an important measure and the House rejects it, the House rejects that Government and the Government goes and another Government comes in its place. It should be clearly understood that this is one of the important measures to which the Government attaches importance and on which it will stand or fall."

Again on 19th of December 1949, the Prime Minister said: "I do not wish the House to think in the slightest degree that we consider that this Hindu Code Bill is not of importance, because we do attach the greatest importance to it, as I said, not because of any particular clause or anything, but because of the basic approach to this vast problem in problems, economic and social. We have achieved political freedom in this country, political independence. That is a stage in the journey, and there are other stages, economic, social and other and if society is to advance, there must be this integrated advance on all fronts."

On the 26th of September 1951, the Prime Minister said: "It is not necessary for me to assure the House of the desire of Government to proceed with this measure in so far as we can proceed with it within possibilities, and so far as we are concerned we consider this matter as adjourned till such time as the next opportunity—I hope it will be in this Parliament—offers itself."

This was after the Prime Minister had announced the dropping of the Bill. Who could not have believed in these pronouncements of the Prime Minister? If I did not think that there could be a difference between the promise and performances of the Prime Minister the fault is certainly not mine. My exit from the Cabinet may not be a matter of much concern to anybody in this country. But I must be true to myself and that can be only by going out. Before I do so I wish to thank my collegues for the kindness and courtesy they have shown to me during my membership of the Cabinet. While I am not resigning my membership of the Parliament I also wish to express my gratitude to Members of Parliament for having shown great tolerance towards me.

10 October 1951 B. R. *Ambedkar*

Index